Asian Honor

Overcoming the Culture of Silence

Sam Louie

WESTBOW
PRESS
A DIVISION OF THOMAS NELSON

ISBN: 978-1-4497-4357-4 (sc)
ISBN: 978-1-4497-4358-1 (e)
ISBN: 978-1-4497-4356-7 (hc)

Library of Congress Control Number: 2012904834

WestBow Press books may be ordered through booksellers or by contacting:

WestBow Press
A Division of Thomas Nelson
1663 Liberty Drive
Bloomington, IN 47403
www.westbowpress.com
1-(866) 928-1240

Printed in the United States of America

WestBow Press rev. date: 04/20/2012

Introduction

ASIAN CULTURES ARE ROOTED in shame. We are known as shame-based cultures since our lives, families, and mindsets revolve around some aspect of shame. Our identities are forged by upholding our honor while trying to avoid any shame-producing feelings, thoughts, or beliefs. Few are able to break the cultural shame that binds them. Instead, they suffer in silence.

I should know, as my life was once shackled by shame. I was hiding and afraid to reveal myself to the world. I was fearful that if anyone really knew me, they would leave me. I believed I could not be loved or accepted as I am. I strove to prove to myself and the world that I was "good enough" by trying to excel at school, sports, career, and my relationships, including my relationship with God. I would never let anyone see my weaknesses, my fears, or my insecurities. It was the Asian way. It was the American way. And, for the most part, I thought it was the only way.

In psychological circles we call this a "false self" because the reality and vitality of life are cut off from the person who refuses to acknowledge any feelings or thoughts that are deemed unacceptable to him or his culture. The false self is a defensive construct that protects the ego for countless millions of people striving to earn their way to approval and acceptance. Unless the false self is confronted and torn down, the individual will stay locked in an emotional prison that will stifle his soul, which craves to be released from bondage.

Part of my work as a therapist now is to help clients tap into their neglected emotional worlds. It's analogous to a personal trainer helping clients with exercise. In therapy, the neglected "muscles" being worked are the emotions. A person learns in childhood that certain emotions are deemed unacceptable; among them may be rage, grief, helplessness, envy, sadness, fear, and sexual desire. Given enough time, the child can learn to associate these feelings with shame.

Shame is pernicious. It will choke a person with the belief that he is bad, defective, and unlovable when these "unacceptable" feelings are aroused later in adulthood. To keep these feelings under control, shame-bound individuals are likely to turn to addictive behaviors, because addictions temporarily ward off unpleasant feelings by altering one's mood.

As I write this book, I'm divorced and in recovery from my own addiction. The list of sources for my shame is long, and I hate feeling exposed, but I know of no other way to help than to share my story with others. This book is dedicated to those looking to break out of their bondage. May you have the courage to step out of darkness and experience the freedom that's possible through intimacy with God and your fellow man.

Chapter 1
Asian Shame And Honor

WHEN YOU THINK OF Asian people, you must remember that Asians are collectivist by culture. Unlike the United States, which prides itself on the individual or "I" factor, Asian nations exalt the "we." As a result, Asian societies are often referred to as "shame-based" cultures in which social order is maintained through the use of shame.

Before I go further into the intricate and negative aspects of Asian shame, I need to acknowledge that shame is best understood by looking at it through the prism of honor. In Asian cultures, the concepts of shame and honor are inextricably tied together. It's like the yin and the yang: they coexist. So to fully grasp Asian shame, we need to understand this tension with honor that's often neglected.

Honor and upholding honor is paramount in Asian cultures. We learn early from our parents that everything we do is predicated on bringing honor to our families: our grades, our achievements, our careers, our marriages, and our children (repeat cycle with them).

"You're Asian; Make Us Proud!"

As a first-generation Chinese American whose parents sacrificed their own livelihoods to give me the opportunity to get an American education, my mantra was to "honor the family" above all else. Growing up in Seattle's tightly knit Asian community meant adhering to the unwritten code to make a good name for myself, and thus my family.

My parents were low-paid restaurant workers (dad was a cook and mom a waitress) who pinned all their hopes on my two younger brothers and me. We were to succeed and fulfill this expectation of filial honor. We had no other choice, lest we end up shaming our family name.

My Family Name

In an Asian family, you learn honor early when your parents tell you about the meaning of your family name and its implications for your life. As a "Louie," my honor, loyalty, and allegiance belonged to the family. What was important in life was not my individual self or accomplishments; instead, everything I did was to be geared toward bringing glory to the family name.

Chinese names are written in three characters, with your family name written first, not last. My Chinese name transliterates as Louie Fu Yuen. So as a child, when Chinese people asked me what my name was, they weren't asking for my American first name to identify me as an individual. They wanted to know who my family was. So I'd answered, "Louie, Fu Yuen."

In China when you first meet someone, this same process occurs. If translated into English, the question would be something like this: "What's your last name?" There isn't a desire to ask for your first name until the questioner can understand you within the larger and richer context of your family's heritage. In answering, I'd say, "I'm a Louie." The person I was speaking with would respond with his or her own family name so that we could get a mutual sense of who we were based on our families' lineages and reputations.

Consequently, as a "Louie" my reputation and honor today are still partly in the hands of my deceased ancestors. If they left a good legacy, then I could find favor within the Chinese community in the present time. The closest American association I can think of that might resemble this linkage to the past is the reverence bestowed upon the Kennedy legacy in the US.

The Oldest Son

When one is the oldest son, the obligation to maintain family honor is even stronger. I am the one responsible for carrying this honor forward to future generations. And as a first-generation Chinese American, the expectation to succeed in this new land only made the burden heavier.

Generations of Asian families have built their successes or failures simply by making use of the family reputation handed down by previous generations. Consequently, as I stepped out into the world of education, career, and marriage, the weight of obligation to bring honor to my family and my ancestral roots was monumental. Anything that could cast a negative light on my name would be seen as dishonorable or a loss of "face" for the family.

Saving Face

Because of the Asian fixation on honor, we learn to do and to achieve as a means to "save face." Face is how one is seen or judged by another in Asian cultures. When people talk about how Asian cultures are shame-based, they're referring to the concern an Asian person has for what others think about him.

If someone "loses face," it creates a deep feeling of humiliation for letting down family, culture, and self. You can see Asian shame in action when an Asian commits suicide. Taking one's own life is seen as an honorable way of atoning for public disgrace and an expression of one's deep sense of shame.

It should also be noted the Chinese character, or *kanji*, for "face" is the same as the character for "mask." If you follow this line of thinking in which your face is known as your mask, it's no wonder why traditional Asian people will do whatever it takes to hide their emotions or their true face by putting on their mask. Since saving face is seen as bringing honor to oneself and one's culture, then hiding one's true feelings also carries a degree of honor. Hence, the outward display of authentic emotions is shunned, since others would view that behavior as a loss of face.

Many Asians will pay any price to maintain face as this becomes the most important aspect of life. Anger, disappointment, sadness, and fear were never expressed or condoned in my family. As a result, my brothers and I unconsciously learned to associate these emotions with shame.

"I'm a bad person"

In a strange and twisted way, my brothers and I internalized becoming authentic to our human experience and emotions as being "bad." With such a belief, when I go through experiences that are not honorable or sources of pride for my family, what then? When you feel you've let down not only yourself, but also your family, your ancestors, and your entire culture, and you can't talk about it with them, it inevitably leads to toxic shame.

This is a shame that seeps into one's veins and courses through one's very being. This deep sense of rejection, humiliation, and failure penetrates one's core and robs one of life. It leads to the view of one's entire self as flawed, defective, unworthy, and ultimately unlovable.

Shame Defined

So what exactly is shame? Is it the same feeling as guilt? People often use the words "shame" and "guilt" interchangeably, but there is a distinction between the two that needs to be recognized if we are to understand the life-draining consequences of shame.

Guilt is healthy because it tells us what mistakes we need to correct and leads us to think of ways to rebuild ourselves and our relationships with others, including God.

Shame, on the other hand, is a perverse and distorted belief that we are bad, that we are inherently unworthy of love. When a person feels shame, instead of wanting to be corrected, he believes he deserves to be persecuted, punished, and tormented. A shame-based person doesn't know how to feel healthy guilt. Instead, he believes that his essential core is "bad" or "defective," and it is that essential badness that is reflected in his thoughts, beliefs, and behaviors.

Guilt for a thought or behavior is usually a feeling of remorse that's directed outwardly, toward another person. You think about how you have impacted another person's thoughts and feelings. There's a sense of constructive sorrow, and with it a love-motivated desire to change that is rooted in concern for others.

Shame is self-centered. It's an internal feeling that's directed at attacking your own soul. You berate yourself. You feel worthless as a person. Given enough time, if a person internalizes shame and can't distinguish it from guilt, the damage is devastating. Shame becomes like a malignant cancer spreading through the individual.

In essence, guilt is our conscience telling us that we may have failed and moves us to change, whereas shame keeps us locked in a cycle of self-absorption and punishment. So here's how to discern the difference: A guilty person fears punishment and wants to make amends. A shame-based person wants to be punished.

Asians growing up in a shame-based environment can become infected with this toxic view of themselves. The toxicity can lead to relief by way of suicide as a means to restore honor to the family.

Chapter 2
Asian Shame And Suicide

SUICIDE HAS LONG BEEN a way to preserve family honor in Asia. This sense that honor can be obtained by suicide was evident among the Japanese kamikaze pilots of World War II. Kamikazes saw their behavior as an act of bravery and sacrifice. Death was seen as success by the kamikaze, as opposed to the disgrace associated with defeat, capture, or surrender.

This tradition of preferring suicide to defeat dates back centuries to feudal Japan, when the samurai reigned. The samurai lived by the Bushidō code, meaning "Way of the Warrior-Knight," whereby the accepted practice was to follow this code of loyalty and honor until death. Consequently the samurai route to glory was through death, associating honor with suicide.

The reason a samurai accepted suicide so readily was that their families instilled in them a strong sense of duty. Not surprisingly, this view of suicide as a means to preserve a family and culture's honor still permeates the Japanese today. According to the World Health Organization, Japan has the highest suicide rate among Asian countries, with more than 30,000 suicides annually according to its most recent report. (World Health Organization, 2009)

Taking one's life is seen as an honorable way of atoning for public disgrace and expression of one's deep sense of shame. "Suicide in Japan, often misunderstood in America, is the ultimate means of taking responsibility for having brought shame to one's group. This most personal act is, in Japan, still an act that expresses a supreme concern for what others think" (Condon 1984, 30).

Yukiko Nishihara, a Japanese suicide prevention activist and founder of the Tokyo chapter of Befrienders Worldwide, offers this cultural explanation to Japanese suicide: "Death puts an end to everything, and the victim becomes a god, and becoming free of criticism" (USA TODAY, 5/29/2007)

Yuzo Kato, the director of the Tokyo Suicide Prevention Centre, believes shame and honor play significant roles that contribute to the high suicide rate. "Japan's national character is such that people are socially conditioned to hide their pain, to avoid troubling others by opening up" (McCurry 2008)

In 2007, Japan's agriculture minister Toshikatsu Matsuoka killed himself while facing investigation over an expenses scandal. In response, the governor of Tokyo, Shintaro Ishihara, glorified Matsuoka, stating he was a true samurai because he had committed suicide to preserve his honor. (Chambers 2010)

However, the climate of social acceptance of suicide in Japan is changing. My brother, who lived in Tokyo for several years, told me the Japanese government is trying to lower the high suicide rate by enacting laws that levy fines against the families of those who commit suicide, as a means to discourage this long-standing practice. Needless to say, the prevalence of Japanese suicides offers a window on the shame-based pressure exerted by a society on its members to uphold honor at any cost.

Chapter 3
Asian Shame And Families

If you don't heal the wounds of your childhood, you bleed into the future.

-Oprah Winfrey

GOD MADE EACH OF us unique. It's hard to repress your thoughts, abilities, and personality, but Asian cultures have found a way to do that by inculcating the belief that we are not to be special or different. Instead, the typical Asian family tries to cultivate obedience, harmony, and cooperation known as "collectivism," whereby many individual Asians lose their sense of selfhood.

Don't Think For Yourself

While the "family first" system may have worked in Asia, the breakdown becomes obvious once Asian families try to assimilate in the United States. Many Asian parents do not recognize the psychological harm they do to their children when those children are not given the appropriate opportunities, in terms of American culture, for human growth and development.

Part of this growth is dependent on parents' willingness to let their kids separate psychologically from them, a process known in therapeutic circles as *individuation*. Children need to know it's safe for them to have their own thoughts and feelings, however uncomfortable or unsettling those are for their parents. Unfortunately, typical Asian parents consider it risky to let kids think on their own or make their own decisions, for fear they'll make the wrong ones and end up dishonoring the family name.

To counter this perceived threat, Asian parents can snuff out their children's emotional development by disregarding their children's thoughts or not giving children space for feedback.

> Families like these do not particularly support individuation and often take attempts of children to separate as assaults on the system. They do not necessarily encourage gradual, healthy separation while maintaining connection. Children separate at the peril of losing their place. (Dayton 2000, 63)

The process of abandoning one's emotions and needs can take years, but once an Asian child learns to repress them, the firm foundation of shame is set. Entrenched in the child's mind is the overarching feeling of shame. No matter what the emotion is, the individual is made to feel bad, unworthy, and wrong for even having it. As a result, the child cuts himself off from his very core. He may appear well-adjusted and agreeable in his attempts to garner parental approval, but his motives are disingenuous. He suffers the fear of being ostracized for having opinions contrary to his family's beliefs or values.

The development of shame originates in childhood. Children learn from their parents how to modulate their emotions and behaviors by a psychological process known as *mirroring*. Just as a mirror reflects an image, parents act as a "mirror" for their children's emotional worlds. Parents have the tremendous responsibility to reflect and thereby validate their children's internal world. A parent may give the child comfort through this acknowledgment, or a parent may disrupt this process by disregarding the child's inner experience.

If parents cannot properly mirror their children's emotions, then the children will have extreme difficulty processing their emotions and may start second-guessing their feelings altogether. Since Asian cultures take pride in stoicism, generations of Asian children have been left wanting, in terms of emotional validation and expression.

> Because of the traditional hierarchical and vertical structure of Asian American families prohibiting free verbal expression of emotions, especially true thoughts and negative feelings, family members may not be equipped with the communication skills to discuss problems and to express themselves openly in a family group setting. For example, for parents to discuss their "adult" problems or to express sadness in front of the children is considered highly inappropriate and is viewed as losing control. (McGoldrick, Garcia-Preto, and Nydia 2005, 284)

What a child internalizes from this lack of mirroring is abandonment. Abandonment is the destructive seed that takes root in a child's soul and leads to shame. Like a violin that's not in tune with the rest of the orchestra, parents who are out of tune with their child's emotions stand a good chance of leaving a child feeling isolated and emotionally abandoned, not just in childhood but also in adulthood.

Abandonment is more than a parents' inability to mirror their children's emotions. This feeling of helplessness can also come from physical abandonment, emotional neglect, criticism, and abuse in any form. The underlying messages that children receive from being abandoned are those of "I'm not wanted," "I'm unlovable," and "I cannot depend on anyone for my survival."

All of these feelings of shame can begin as early as infancy, since this is the time when the child is learning how to trust and form an emotional bond with the mother. But this bond is not automatic. The mother must do more than just feed the infant. She must enter his emotional world. No matter how affluent or educated a mother is, she can still lack the skills to do this properly.

> Biological birth does not guarantee a relationship between infant and parent—mother or father. Both parent

and child experience feelings, needs, and expectations in relationship to the other. What conveys the parent's desire to have a relationship is expressed *interest* in entering the child's experiential world, which the child will eventually reciprocate.

More importantly, the child experiences that the relationship is actually wanted by the parent. Birth alone does not satisfy the need for relationship. Each child needs to feel wanted and thereby experientially know with certainty that he or she is special. (Kaufman 1996, 65-66)

Can you "feel" how the infant must experience being wanted by his caregivers for this bonding to occur? Can you see how critical this nonverbal phase is in establishing a healthy attachment to the child?

This need for healthy infant attachment cannot be brushed over or minimized. Much of the work in therapy involves undoing the trauma of a ruptured relationship with one's primary caregivers. We call it *re-parenting*, in which, as a therapist, I must try and establish an emotional bond with my client that was lacking from his childhood. If re-parenting is to be successful, the client must have a corrective emotional experience during which he can internalize the feeling that I genuinely care about him. He must "feel" that I want to know him. Everything from his thoughts and feelings to his hopes and fears must be explored so he can learn to trust me at his core, thereby establishing the groundwork for a relationship based on true emotional intimacy.

Self-Esteem Is "Other" Esteem

People often throw out loaded phrases to describe another person, such as "She has good self-esteem" or "He's insecure," without recognizing that terms like security in one*self*, *self*-worth, and *self*-esteem are misleading. How a person gauges his worth is dependent on how *others* view him. Self-worth is actually "other-worth." His self-esteem is formed by how others have esteemed him since birth. People can pretend there is security in money, good looks, achievement, grades, or status, but a more accurate barometer of one's worth is how one is esteemed in relationship to one's primary caregivers.

Take, for example, an adult man who finds himself in therapy due to a pattern of emotionally abusive relationships. The women he chooses always neglect his needs by withdrawing from him, criticizing him, and attacking him. When I as his therapist pull back the layers, I invariably can see the association between his family upbringing and his current relational crisis.

> I knew this man had come from a large family where his two exhausted parents worked hard, always worried about money, and seemed overwhelmed. He rarely felt worthwhile or important in his family, so he rarely felt worthwhile or important in himself. He said, "The worst thing was I never felt they enjoyed me. I hunger to be enjoyed." (Halpern 1982, 59)

Family Ruptures

In my own family, my middle brother was neglected very early in life. My mother gave birth to him ten months after giving birth to me. Later, she confided to me that she had postpartum depression after his birth. In addition, she and my father were struggling financially in Hong Kong and lived in a small, one-bedroom flat. With few resources and no more than middle school educations, my parents uprooted themselves from Hong Kong. At the age of thirty-one and twenty-seven, they left the security of their native Chinese culture and language to move to Seattle, in the hope of providing a better life for me and my two younger brothers.

The acculturation process was arduous. Neither of my parents knew a word of English. Mom acknowledged she took out some of her frustration on my middle brother. I'm told she deliberately put hot food in his mouth when he was an infant, while he cried profusely. Even though my parents never spoke any words to indicate that my brother was not loved, these early experiences of not feeling wanted carried over from childhood to adulthood.

I considered myself a latchkey kid who learned to survive and become self-reliant. Lacking the opportunity to enjoy my parents in play or recreation fostered my belief that I would need to fend for myself and never depend on anyone. On many wet, dreary, overcast days in Seattle, I found refuge on the playground, playing basketball alone as a way to insulate myself from my loneliness and the disconnection from my family. The days eventually turned to years, during which I spent endless hours shooting hoops as an escape from the misery of life.

The misery I'm referring to was not one of physical neglect but of lack of relationship. It was excruciating to be at home with parents with whom I could not connect, so I figured I'd be better off playing basketball. What I truly wanted was family—a family I could connect with emotionally.

The Family I Never Had

As a boy, the first media image that left an indelible image in my heart was a Mormon television commercial broadcast in the 80s. The commercial gripped me as a ten-year-old boy. Thirty years later, I can still shed tears just visualizing it. The commercial showed an idyllic outdoor scene of a father and son playing catch.

Why was that scene so powerful? If taken at face value, it really was nothing more than an activity between father and son. But at its deepest level, I believe that image speaks to every boy's yearning to be known, cherished, loved, and connected to his father. I longed for those moments but knew they weren't possible in a family system that made emotional isolation an unwritten rule of life.

This sense of living life separately from my family continued in middle and high school. Consequently I jumped at any and every opportunity to escape home. I got a paper route and delivered newspapers every day. I rode the bus with my friends on the weekends. I joined an Asian American basketball league. I was part of a Chinese American church. I played endless hours of video games at the local minimart. I went anywhere where I could get away from my family. When I saw other friends hanging out with their brothers or sisters, I could only wonder why. I wanted nothing to do with my brothers or my parents. I wanted a life separate from those who should have been closest to me, and saw that separation as the path toward independence.

My Disconnected Adult Family

As adults now, my brothers and I try to stay connected by playing basketball or sending an occasional e-mail to each other. However, the years of distancing and disconnectedness can't be forgotten. In fact, the scars remain fresh.

When my youngest brother got married in 2009, my middle brother shared his feelings of childhood abandonment during one of the nights we were all hanging out. He viewed me as stuck on blaming our parents, while I saw the need for acknowledging our pain and disappointment as an essential path toward healing. You can see from our e-mail exchanges how past, hidden hurts in our family continue to fester.

Sam—

I'm not the only person that thought you were "selfish" and insecure about yourself that you must blame me, our parents, and probably the world for not providing you the emotional "love" that you seek. Shoot, I wish our parents gave us affection and love but they didn't. Also, I wish all three of us bonded when our parents weren't able to provide it, but we didn't. Sure we had it rough since we never really bonded at all. Well, I believe we must just work slowly and hope for the best. See you.
Ken L

Ken,

I DON'T blame our parents. I understand the good aspects that they brought into my life but I can also acknowledge where they have let me down tremendously instead of pretending everything was great.

Honestly, the past will always be a part of your life unless you learn to work through some of the past issues. Why do you think you even brought them up the first night we went out? I wasn't the one asking you about that. You just shared with the group without any prompting that, "I cried myself to sleep, had suicidal thoughts and had no love".

I appreciate you for reaching out to me and yes bonding takes a long time since it was never properly done. Keep in mind, if our parents couldn't bond with us, then it's very difficult for siblings to learn how to do that with each other. Once again, not blaming but just recognizing the difficulties of trying to learn America by ourselves.
Sam

As it stands, we're communicating again, but I'm careful to keep things superficial as the wounds of the past can erupt at any time if I delve too deeply. It's unfortunate, because what I see and hear is unprocessed shame at the core of many of my brother's issues: the shame in feeling he wasn't wanted by our parents; the shame in refusing to acknowledge any feelings of hurt toward our parents in an attempt to stay in denial. This inability to speak honestly about his heartache and brokenness only submerges him deeper into the pit of shame.

> When a child consistently fails to experience this distinct, individualized relationship, shame is generated because the interpersonal bridge is ruptured. The impact of parental actions *convinces* the child that he or she either counts as a person or instead is not wanted. Consider more closely how shame is generated in a dysfunctional parent-child relationship. There are a number of critical patterns. One arises when either or both parents do not actually want the child or instead desire a child of the opposite sex. Such rejection can be clear and open, ambivalent and hidden, entirely unconscious, or defended against by over-possessiveness and over-protectiveness. Resentment toward the child will inevitably find expression, however secret, leaving the child feeling responsible for not belonging. (Kaufman 1996, 66)

No family deliberately sets out to create a fertile breeding ground for shame. It exists because of unconscious rules of impaired communication that are perpetuated from one generation to the next, referred to as generational patterns. These rules govern stability in the family, and any attempt to change these rules is met with resistance.

Most clients in therapy repeatedly received messages that denied their feelings and invalidated their experience. Some examples of these messages include:

- You shouldn't feel that way.
- Why would a silly thing like that make you mad?
- We don't talk about those things.
- You can't possibly be hungry now.
- How can you be tired? You've hardly done anything.
- You shouldn't be upset at your mother. She loves you very much.
- You don't really want to talk about that.
- What's the matter with you? How could you feel that way!
(Teyber 2006, 54)

In emotionally disconnected families, when children express a feeling or thought, their parents simply ignore them, thus invalidating the children's experiences. Consistent invalidation over time has long-lasting consequences that some authors have described as "soul murder" because children lose their voices to express any feeling. As adults, they enter therapy because they have lost their abilities to say no, articulate what they want or need, set boundaries with others, or even acknowledge feeling hurt or sad.

When their subjective experience has been denied repeatedly, clients do not know what they are feeling, what they like or value, or what they want to do. Denying the validity of their own experience, these clients characteristically say to themselves, "Oh, nothing really happened"; "It wasn't that bad"; or "It doesn't really matter" when it actually was significant to them. (Teyber 2006, 55)

This reaction is even more acute within the Asian household, since the individual is sacrificed for the sake of the family.

An unhealthy relational dynamic manifests itself in two unwritten rules:

1. *No talking rule ("Children should be seen and not heard")*

Talking is limited to superficial matters (e.g., food, weather, grades, etc.). Anything pertaining to thoughts, concerns, desires, feelings, and real needs are suppressed so that the appearance of harmony can be maintained in the family.

2. *No feeling rule*

In traditional Asian households, parents are the ultimate authority, not only in childhood but also in adulthood. This turns the family from a dynamic and open system into an authoritarian, closed system in which the parents are always right and there's no room for disagreement or discussion of other viewpoints. Parents beat emotional submission into their kids. Children are limited to a yes or no pattern of relating to their parents. Under this system, it becomes ingrained that children's thoughts, opinions, and feelings do not mean anything to their parents. This leads to shame, resentment, and sometimes rebellion.

Asian parents typically do not allow the free expression of anger, sadness, fear, disappointment, or other "negative" emotions, ironically as a way of helping their children cope. Parents believe that by not talking about these matters, they are doing a service to their children. Unfortunately, when emotions are buried, it's like a volcano slowly building up pressure. One day it can erupt, causing catastrophic damage in the form of addictive behaviors.

Having parents who just tolerate emotional expression is not enough to eliminate shame. Emotions must be encouraged, nurtured, and worked through. Parents must take an active role in asking how a child feels and giving appropriate feedback.

Think about a child who cries out in panic because he fears his mom doesn't want him. If the terror-stricken child is allowed to cry but his fears of abandonment are not assuaged, the child learns subconsciously that his mother doesn't care about him and that he must fend for himself in this world. If a boy comes home distraught because he's been teased, bullied, or beat up at school, and his parents do not ask him about his day or notice his sense of dejection, this will only add to the boy's internal feeling that he's unwanted or worthless. Whether parents directly tell children not to cry or indirectly do so by ignoring the tears, the message is the same. Children internalize that these emotions are "bad" and avoid sharing them, thinking they must be inherently defective as well for having such feelings.

Chapter 4
Asian Shame And Addiction

IN ADDITION TO ITS connection with emotions, shame can also be linked to needs and desires. Basic human needs such as the need for human touch, the need for relationships, the need for personal interaction with our loved ones, and the need for affirmation can be thwarted in childhood. When parents do not display physical signs of affection (e.g., hugs or kisses), provide verbal affirmation such as words of encouragement, or take the time to know their children individually, these children will seek solace elsewhere. Their drive to meet these core intimacy needs will be insatiable, and can lead to the obsessive use of drugs, alcohol, gambling, shopping, work, sports, sex, or food. They may exist in an emotional black hole, where they think, "I'm not good enough," leaving many empty, alone, afraid, and hopelessly drowning in shame or compulsive and addictive behaviors.

Mother Wounds

I remember a time in the seventh grade when a friend asked me if I would like to help him on his once-a-week paper route. I thought this would be a fun way to make some money, but when I asked my mom for permission, the answer was simply no, end of discussion. I was doing well in school, so I was baffled by her quick and decisive response. I was frustrated by her answer and internalized that my voice didn't matter. She did not explain how she reached her decision or help me process my anger. The experience left me feeling shame for trying to assert some independence by asking for a paper route.

This type of family dynamic in which there is limited flexibility in the family rules leads either to submission or rebellion. A child may submit by deciding simply to obey, denying and cutting off major aspects of his or her humanity to avoid being the target of discipline. Or a child may eventually rebel out of a natural desire to grow toward psychological and physical independence from the parents.

I eventually rebelled a year after my mother decided against the paper route. For the first time, I openly challenged her authority. I felt my request for a paper route was legitimate, so I asserted my need by helping another friend with his daily paper route. I don't remember asking for permission or caring what she thought. I just did it. Despite getting what I wanted, the shadow of shame cast its pall over me because of my defiance against her wishes.

"The Nail That Sticks Up Gets Hammered Down"

There's an old Japanese proverb that goes something like this: "The nail that sticks up gets hammered down." For Asian children, the desire for individuation and autonomy is often met with resistance in traditional households. Parents in this system typically do not encourage children to think on their own, as it would cause too much distress for the parents. It is easier for parents to assert their control over children and ignore children's needs, wants, and feelings.

When parents do so, the children lose an authentic connection and never learn a valuable life lesson in how human relationships can help relieve anxiety. Instead, these children become prime candidates for addiction later in life, looking for nonrelational ways to assuage their emotional distress.

Here's a story about a woman who dealt with the death of her husband through gambling and its trance-like effects:

> "Gambling allowed me to be with people without really being with them," said one compulsive gambler, whose acting out became uncontrollable after her husband died. The trance salved her grief and sorrow. It filled up her

emptiness. She felt no pain as long as she was in the casino. Addiction and the trance offered her a solution, and she used it as long as her savings and insurance monies held out. Then she was forced to confront the reality of her losses, and the blow was even more devastating. Not only had she lost her husband but also the money they had put aside to support her. Addiction takes and takes, and then takes some more. (Nakken 1996, 4-5)

Father Wounds

In healthy families, a son wants to delight in his father. This was true for me growing up. I would relish the opportunity to give my dad a massage. I also wanted to be his little helper when I noticed him doing handyman chores around the house. But this feeling was not reciprocated. The first memorable wound from my father came during my elementary school years when I saw him outside painting. I scrambled up to him, buoyed with wide-eyed anticipation that I would be allowed to help. Instead, he shooed me away. I was devastated. I just wanted to soak in my father's presence. It may not sound like much, but to a ten-year-old boy filled with a desire to connect with his father, I heard a not-so-subtle message—I was not wanted. One incident isn't enough to scar a child, but enough of these types of encounters will lead to the internalization of this belief.

Years later in high school, another desire to connect with my dad stirred in me. I had invited him to watch me play in a basketball game as part of our Chinese basketball league. Other Chinese parents would be there and I thought it would be nice for him to support me. He attended the game, but while I was playing, I glanced over and saw him reading a Chinese newspaper. My heart sank. I truly wanted his praise. Basketball was the one activity I was good at, and I wanted him to see that.

After that, I retreated within and vowed never to ask my father for support. Little did I know, my heart would harden from that day forward. I learned how to keep people at a safe distance so I would never have to depend on others and face the possibility of getting hurt or disappointed.

Parental Impact On My Own Relationships

Because of the emotional void between me and my parents, this same pattern of relating became evident in many of my romantic relationships with women. The idea of trusting women became fused with the trauma of abandonment. This meant I was attracted to women who would abandon me. This pattern was unconscious, and I would not recognize it until years later when it was uncovered in therapy.

It was no surprise I chose the women I chose. I was not connected to many of the women I dated early on in college, nor did I want to be. I never wanted them to know me. It was more comfortable being distant, similar to what I had experienced growing up. Yet the woman I eventually chose as my marriage partner was a woman who triggered those early childhood abandonment fears of not being wanted.

Early on, when I first started dating my now ex-wife, I remember being gripped with fear at the prospect of losing her after she told me she could not date me any longer. She said it was due to our cultural differences: she was Korean and I was Chinese. She explained that her parents would not approve and she would have to end our three-week courtship.

Instead of being disappointed and sad, I remember feeling paralyzed by the sheer prospect of being alone. I refused to let her go. I begged and demanded she stay with me, like a desperate child clinging to his mother's side. Much later in therapy, I would learn this was not an adult love but an infantile love based on fear. I was essentially a little boy trapped in a man's body.

> If the childhood need to be admired and confirmed is frustrated, it is intensified into a lasting craving. The child grows to adulthood with a piece close to the heart left behind. These people look like grown-ups, but the tenuous quality of their selfhood leaves them with child-like dependency on others for reassure and praise ... they are obsessed with the opinion of others and have an inordinate need to be loved and admired. (Nichols 1987, 148-149)

The relationship didn't end but blossomed into a marriage. Yet it felt like a child-parent relationship in which I was a child who could only "take" from her. I saw myself as an emotional vacuum cleaner, constantly sucking her dry. I had a black hole in my heart and I was hoping she could fill it. I constantly looked to her to fill my needs and could never reciprocate in kind. As John Bradshaw describes it, "They have a hole in their soul created by unresolved grief and developmental dependency deficits. This makes them adult children. Needy children need parents, so adult children turn lovers into parents, someone to take care of their needs" (Bradshaw 2005, 46-47).

This dysfunctional, child-adult relationship would eventually crush my hopes of a lifelong marriage as I looked for other ways to fill the hole in my heart. I focused on my career in television news. That didn't work. I diverted my attention to watching and playing sports, yet there was still a deep ache in my heart. Then I stumbled onto pornography, and that became the salve for my pain.

Chapter 5
My Shame And Addiction

A Shattered Dream

I BELIEVE IF WE'RE honest with ourselves, a point comes in each of our lives when we encounter what I describe as a "shattered dream." This is when your deepest desires or yearnings in life collide with the reality of failure, disgrace, disappointment, or shame. The moment can arise from a failed relationship, getting fired, a rupture in the family, or an injury or health condition that forever impacts your life.

For myself, it came abruptly when I was thirty-one years old. Until then, life was a blur of fun, excitement, and upward progress. In five short years as a television news reporter, I went from working in a small Montana town with no money for rent or groceries to working in Los Angeles, the media capital of the world. A typical day could include rubbing shoulders with Hollywood stars like Will Smith at a movie premiere. I believed I was on top of the world both professionally and personally. At the time, I was married and thought I was invincible. I was planning to live a "normal" life by starting a family, going on nice vacations, buying a home, and even going to church. I was that certain of my future and destiny.

Never did I foresee what would happen next. I was taken from the comfort of a nurturing marital and family life and thrust into the harsh reality of living on my own after getting slapped with divorce papers.

This was a brutal shock to me, a severe jolt to my system. Everything I knew, valued, or thought about life came to a crashing end. During this tumultuous period, I groped in darkness, searching for meaning and purpose. All aspects my life had to be re-evaluated: career, marriage, childhood, parents, religion, even my emotional makeup (or lack thereof). Nothing was off-limits. I wanted answers and understanding to bring healing to my deepest wounds. I went to individual counseling and seminars, and read countless books about relationships.

What I learned from this process was how much pride existed in my heart prior to the divorce. Up to that time, I believed I controlled everything and wouldn't let God in on any of it. Relationally, I saw myself as "better" than others who were divorced, single, uneducated, or working in unsatisfying jobs, as well as those who weren't Christian. I simply believed if they had patterned their lives after mine and worked hard enough, then they too could have a successful marriage, a good family, and joy in their careers.

Like a gardener tending to his plants, I spent years cultivating my pride. But my pride quickly withered with the soul-crushing pronouncement that my wife found me lacking as a man. I was stunned. What had gone wrong?

It came as a shock to my family and friends when my wife decided to divorce me. We looked so good together. We shared the same sense of humor. We came from families that each valued marriage and togetherness. After the breakup became official, I became adept at answering questions, pointing to our lack of communication, lack of intimacy, and cultural issues, but one element was rarely discussed. With the exception of my pastor and therapist, I harbored a secret I dared not share with anyone else—I was an addict. Not a typical alcohol or drug addict, but someone who was addicted to sex.

I craved sex and the feelings of comfort and control it gave me. It was not evident to me until my sex life with my wife had dried up after four years of marriage. I would joke to her that I needed to schedule an appointment with her for sex. She would laugh, but inside I was seething because I didn't know what to do. How could I talk about my disappointment? How could I talk about my desires?

Instead of having an open dialogue, I decided to take matters into my own hands by turning to pornography. For countless nights after I returned home late from work, I went online and looked at porn while she slept. It became a ritual.

"Thank God, I'm Caught"

One night while I was caught in my trance, she woke up to use the restroom. She peered into the living room and saw me looking at porn on the computer. A loud shriek of disgust pierced the silence of the night. My body shook as I felt exposed, helpless, alone, and afraid; a whirlwind of mixed feelings coursed through me. I intuitively knew my marriage was in jeopardy, yet there was also a huge sigh of relief. "Thank God!" I thought. I was relieved she had caught me, as I was tired of living my double life. Finally someone knew my secret.

Despite my terror that evening, I also felt a sense of peace as the years of guilt, shame, and silence came to light. A tremendous burden had been lifted; I could not hide behind denial or rationalizations. I had to acknowledge to her and to myself that the tentacles of lust, infatuation, and pornography had strangled all the intimacy in our marriage.

The feelings of loss, abandonment, and shame associated with my divorce under these circumstances were excruciating. How could this happen to me? Nothing was more important to me than my marriage; not my career, not my family, not my relationship with God. Nothing was more important than my desire to uphold the Asian honor of a good marriage.

The cultural shame was compounded by religious shame. I belonged to an Asian-American church. Everything that I believed in about a Christian marriage had disintegrated in front of my eyes. How could this happen when we were Christians? I didn't know much about the Bible or Christianity at the time, but I was certain God was against divorce. Disillusionment with my faith quickly set in. I felt like a failure not just to myself but to others. I felt like a failure in the eyes of my immediate family, my grandparents, my deceased ancestors, my church, and the Asian community at large.

I felt that my label as a divorcé turned me into a twenty-first century Hester Prynn emblazoned with a scarlet letter for all to see. The stigma within my culture of both the divorce and the addiction pierced my soul. How had this happened? How could I be so weak? God must hate me.

"Breaking News! I Need Help!"

In television news, you may hear the announcer use the term "breaking news" to describe something immediate or urgent that needs to be brought to the public's attention. When I look back on my time in Missoula, Montana, a small college town located on the westernmost edge of the state, I think the headline that best encapsulated my time there was, "Breaking news—I need help!" Only I didn't realize it.

In the cold Montana winter of 1995, I found my first full-time job in television journalism. I started off as a one-man band. I was the reporter, the videographer, and the editor all rolled into one. I even did weather forecasts as a way to garner more on-camera experience. I worked long hours, including weekends.

In return, I received $13,998 per year. I never thought I would be making less money with a college degree than I made during my time as a lifeguard without one. I was making seven dollars an hour, shooting, editing, and writing all my stories. Before I signed my contract, I asked my boss if he could throw in two extra dollars so I could make an even fourteen thousand, but he shrugged his shoulders and said, "Sam, you know I can't do that." I quickly realized this was not the glamorous life I had envisioned.

Still, the work was itself was exciting. Every day was a new story. Every day meant going to a different location and talking to different people. The city was nestled in a gorgeous valley surrounded by beautiful mountains and wildlife. Bears were often caught rummaging through trash in residential neighborhoods. The beauty, though, was a stark contrast to my internal bleakness and turmoil as a young man driven to make it in his professional career.

I was living alone for the first time, more than five hundred miles away from home., I could not drive back to Seattle at a whim's notice, as I could during college. I was lonely and wracked with insecurity. I questioned my abilities.

It was also the first time I experienced so many bewildering emotions: fear, inadequacy, and culture shock. I was the only Asian guy I knew in the city, or the state for that matter. I wondered to myself, "What if I don't succeed in this career? Will my parents or friends accept me or will they reject me and want nothing to do with me?" I reasoned to myself that failing was not an option. The fear and potential shame of bringing dishonor on myself, my family, my grandparents, and my ancestors weighed heavily on my conscience. I had to succeed.

The anxiety that fueled these questions, doubts, and concerns swirled through my being. Even if I had wanted to talk about it, communication with home wasn't an option. This was before the age of e-mail and cell phones. Some coworkers had long-distance telephone service, but I wanted to save money and chose isolation instead. The isolation sealed my distorted belief that, much like during my childhood, I could not truly trust anyone in my deepest time of need. I would have to tackle these adult challenges alone.

"Better Off Dead"

My work as a cub reporter sucked. My voice was anxious and my presentation was horrible. I was so nervous being on camera that I had the perpetual "deer caught in headlights" look. People would call the station after my live bloopers and wonder what was wrong. In addition, I knew nothing about ethics. I would send my underage intern to buy alcohol at stores, thinking I was doing a public service, only to end up in my boss's office the following morning. Basically, if anything could go wrong in TV news, I did it.

How would I ever get better? Would I be stuck in Montana forever? I could not imagine ever improving. My despair was so strong that I distinctly remember telling myself I'd be better off dead rather than returning home a failure in the eyes of my family and friends. So I forged ahead for a full year in Missoula, Montana, keeping all my fears, insecurities, and frustrations to myself.

But the ferocity of these fear-provoking feelings would not go away. Never did I conceive of discussing them with my parents or friends, as that would signal weakness and shame on my part. I told myself, "I am a man and I am not supposed to show vulnerability or feel fear." Yet the fear of failure gripped me. I struggled mightily to prevent those emotions from overwhelming and paralyzing me.

I needed an outlet. I needed a way out of this pain, something that would be dependable and pleasurable. The answer was sex. The isolation, fears, and loneliness proved to be a perfect storm for the making of my addiction.

Without a girlfriend, I needed sexual release. In the beginning, I found it in traditional rental movies that were a bit racy or had steamy sex scenes. Then I craved more and eventually built up the courage to drive to an adult store. Everything was a blur. I went in, picked out a magazine or two, and left. I didn't make eye contact with anyone for fear that someone would recognize me from watching the local news. All the while, I was disgusted at myself and thought I was perverted to have to resort to this sort of thing. Never did I realize that pornography was an emotional escape from the hardships of life; I only knew it was my source of solace as a single man living alone with no connections.

When I found a girlfriend, the desire for pornography subsided. I didn't think I had any problem because I stopped using pornography while I was with her. I now realize porn and sex were interchangeable for me. Even though I wasn't using porn, I was using sex with her as a coping mechanism. The high of sexual release drowned out any fears I had. I was so disconnected.

After a year of working hard in Montana, I found a better-paying reporter position in Toledo, Ohio. I was now going to be a full-fledged reporter without having to lug around a heavy camera or do any editing. This station had its own photographers, and I would be solely responsible for interviewing, writing, and reporting the news.

Before moving, I had to end my relationship with my girlfriend. I can still recall her crying about our breakup during dinner. I was perplexed and wondered what all the emotional fuss was about. There was no sadness on my part. "Nothing personal; it's just business," I thought.

At the time, I did not see myself as someone who could impact another person. I had spent my childhood trying to engage my parents in a real relationship, but to no avail. So I could not comprehend that my life actually meant something to anyone, especially a woman I had only known for a year. No one ever told me I was special and wanted. I saw myself as replaceable. Worse yet, that is how I viewed her and the other women in my life. I had no recognition of my own inherent worth. To believe I had value in her eyes would have challenged twenty-five years of my Asian upbringing; it was not something I could comprehend.

"Holy Toledo!"

So with my twin-sized mattress and a few other belongings tossed in a small U-Haul trailer, I ventured east to Toledo. I was so excited to leave Montana that I drove twenty-seven hours over the course of two days and arrived in Ohio on the third day. I'm not sure what the rush was all about, because by the time I met my new coworkers, they tempered my enthusiasm with jokes about the city. My colleagues informed me that Toledo was considered the armpit of the state. They may have been correct. The crowning jewel of the city was the Jeep factory. At the time, it manufactured the nation's Wranglers and Cherokees.

The industrial, blue-collar work ethic was reflected in the stories I covered. I reported on more stories about strikes, unions, and local bargaining than I care to remember. In addition, much like Missoula, Toledo was not a cultural hub where Asian Americans flocked. Once again, I was breaking new cultural and professional ground as I became the first Asian man hired by the local media.

Shortly after getting settled, anxiety set in. Starting a new job, now in a new city two thousand miles away from home, meeting new coworkers, brought forth more insecurity. Could I do this? The job paid more than twice what I had been making in Montana, and I was expected to do live news reports with additional responsibilities. This was a lot of stress, as I had only gone live twice before. In

Toledo, I would be required to do live shots multiple times a day, with the fear of making on-air mistakes hovering over me. Once again, to take the edge away, I turned to sex.

The Internet at this time was still in its nascent phase of dial-up service, so visual online pornography wasn't even conceivable. I gravitated back to trolling the bars for women. It really didn't matter who she was or what she did or valued so long as she wanted to have sex with me. I found a woman who became my girlfriend, but I didn't really want to be with her because she was a smoker. I was willing to compromise my values—in fact, I didn't have any. I needed her for sex, and she was the means to that end. The relationship didn't last long; she ended it after two months.

Basketball—My New Fix

I decided to take a break from women to build a healthier lifestyle by going to the gym and playing basketball. However, what started as a seemingly healthy outlet quickly turned into an obsession. Since I was miserable and lonely, I played basketball up to three hours a day, five days a week to pass the time.

But basketball wasn't enough, and eventually the desire for sexual pleasure reappeared. I wasn't having much sex, and took it personally that women in Toledo didn't like Asian guys. With a void in my heart, I needed a quick escape and went back to pornography. This time, with my visibility heightened as a news reporter in a bigger city, I didn't dare walk into an adult bookstore. Instead, I resorted to my old collection of magazines.

"Hi, I Work For ABC News!"

Despite the isolation of working in a city with no friends or family, the television news industry provided some camaraderie and community. Single coworkers would band together and go out to explore the city. One night, we all went to an upscale jazz club. We were just hanging out and enjoying the night when I saw an Asian couple walk in. They were dressed up from attending a wedding. Since this was the first time I'd seen an Asian couple in either

Montana or Ohio, I decided to introduce myself. It was simply an attempt to bond with other Asians.

When I realized the woman was single, I decided to pour on my TV charm. Since I had come straight from work, I had my ABC network lapel on my suit jacket and introduced myself to her with, "Hi, I'm Sam Louie with the ABC news station here in town!" It worked and she agreed to a first date.

On that first date, I cooked a chicken dinner for her. She later told me that what she remembered was not the meal but the conversation. Apparently, I was bitter about getting dumped by my ex (the smoker) and wouldn't stop talking about it. Despite our inauspicious first date, it eventually led to a two-year courtship, culminating in a four-year marriage.

Premarital Counseling: "Do More Porn!"

Before we got married, we had to get premarital counseling, as she had grown up in a Korean Christian family. During this time, we saw a psychologist who questioned us about various aspects of our individual and family backgrounds. Sometime during these sessions, I disclosed my porn habit. The psychologist didn't think there was much of a problem, and he suggested a psychological technique known as "flooding" to rid me of my interest in it. There are success stories in which parents "flood" their children with alcohol to the point of sickness, so the children learn to associate sickness with alcohol and become averse to it. In my case, the psychologist suggested I look at as much pornography as much as possible before I got married as a way to eradicate my interest.

I couldn't believe what I was hearing. I was giddy with excitement. I eagerly followed his "prescription" and my wife thought I was cured. Meanwhile, my secret sexual desires kick-started my shame cycle.

Chapter 6
The Shame Cycle

ONCE SHAME IS ATTACHED to a person's sense of being, the pernicious cycle begins where the self-inflicted wound to the soul is repeated through the creation of an internal shame spiral.

> When an individual suddenly is enmeshed in shame, the focus turns inward and the experience becomes totally internal, frequently with visual imagery present. Shame feelings and their accompanying thoughts flow in a circle, endlessly triggering each other. The event that activated shame is typically relived over and over internally through imagery, causing the sense of shame to deepen and to absorb other neutral experiences that happened before as well as those that may come later, until finally the self is engulfed. Shame becomes paralyzing. (Kaufman 1996, 90)

Shame-bound experiences that limit emotional, mental, and physical expression will eventually recreate shame to encompass the entire soul. Whether you're an addict or not, you've experienced the high that comes when your mood changes because of exercise, food, sex, gambling, work, or shopping, to name a few. For the addict, the intensity of that high is what they live for to block the feelings of shame. In times of anxiety or discomfort, instead of turning to others for relational support, addicts return to this high. They believe it's their true source of comfort and control.

Intoxicating experiences bring the knowledge that through a relationship with an object or event, one's feelings can change. People turn toward addictive or compulsive behavior when they don't like the way they're feeling, and they seek out a mood-changing experience. Nevertheless, in turning to an object or event for relief, one finds the basic illusion upon which addiction is based: finding relief through objects. (Nakken 1996, 2)

When this happens in an addict, he substitutes the intensity of the high for intimacy, self-esteem, support, or a sense of belonging and connection. Since addicts have never experienced intimacy or trust through open and accepting relationships, the addictive behavior or substance naturally fills that void.

We separate addictions into two categories: behavioral and chemical addictions. Chemical addictions can occur when one ingests substances into the body, such as alcohol or drugs. Behavioral addictions stem from compulsive behaviors. A range of behaviors can lead to addiction, such as gambling, work, sex, playing video games, watching TV, and even seemingly healthy outlets like exercise, if it's used in lieu of relationships to cope with one's feelings.

The addiction functions primarily as an escape from intense or overwhelming negative affect—shame alone, shame conjoined with other negative affects, or any negative affect. Whenever feelings of shame are encountered, they can be reduced by becoming addicted to something. Addiction sedates intense negative affect. (Kaufman 1996, 123)

The pain can include anxiety, fear, anger, sadness, or any shame-provoking feelings, thoughts, behaviors, or events. We turn to the addictions to "self-medicate" and numb out those feelings that we consider "bad" and "shameful." But the truth is these feelings never go away. As they reappear, the addict finds alternatives to expressing these shame-bound emotions. The addict is desperately looking for ways to be real and authentic, but the addiction is as close as he can get.

Addictions help us deal with our shame; the two go hand in hand. Often, people compartmentalize addictions and don't address the issue of shame. But unless we can get people out of their shame-bound tendencies, the addictions rarely go away. We must address shame when addressing addictions.

The cycle from shame to addiction is vicious. First, shame-bound people feel an emotion they find intolerable, and internalize it as "bad." To rid themselves of this feeling, they will look for the most pleasurable way out that they can consistently depend on. They often turn to repetitive behaviors or to substances to ward off the painful feeling. As the previous quotation from Nakken indicates, however, "in turning to an object or event for relief, one finds the basic illusion upon which addiction is based: finding relief through objects" (Nakken 1996, 21).

When engaging in the addiction, a neurological high occurs. But once the high is gone, shame eventually sets in. Addicts hold critical and negative self-images because they cannot stop their addictive behaviors despite a desire to do so. For shame-bound addicts, any respite from addiction is short-lived. By going back to their compulsivity, their hearts sink deeper into despair and they may wallow in more shame until they recognize their lives have become unmanageable.

However, if an addict can make an acknowledgment of powerlessness to himself and others, that admission becomes, paradoxically, the first step toward recovery. This is when reality sets in and denial to self is broken.

So what's the difference between a seemingly harmless drink, a large wager at the casino, or our innately human desire for sex when compared to an addiction? Dr. Patrick Carnes is an addiction specialist who details the addiction cycle as a progression of four distinct stages. Even though the addiction cycle described below refers specifically to sex, it also applies to any kind of compulsive behavior.

Preoccupation—the trance or mood wherein the addicts' minds are completely engrossed with thoughts of sex. This mental state creates an obsessive search for sexual stimulation.

Ritualization—the addicts' own special routines that lead up to the sexual behavior. The ritual intensifies the preoccupation, adding arousal and excitement.

Compulsive sexual behavior—the actual sex act, which is the end goal of the preoccupation and ritualization. Sexual addicts are unable to control or stop this behavior.

Depression/despair—addicts feel deep shame. For many, this dark emotion brings on depression or a chronic feeling of hopelessness. One easy way to cure feelings of despair/depression is to start obsessing again. The cycle then perpetuates itself. (Carnes 2001, 167-168)

In addition to the addictive cycle, Carnes notes there are four core beliefs that sex addicts hold to be true.

1. *I am basically a bad, unworthy person.*
2. *No one would love me as I am.*
3. *My needs are never going to be met if I have to depend on other people.*
4. *Sex is my most important need (addicts) , or sex is the most important sign of love (co-addicts). (Carnes 2001, 167-168)*

I was struck by these apparently simple, yet deeply true formulations. In thinking about them at length, I arrived at some insights. Let's take a look at each of these.

1. *I am basically a bad, unworthy person.*

This one hits right at the core of the addict's self-esteem. The addict tends to believe deep down that he is fundamentally flawed. Experiences and formative relationships in his life have led him to this belief. Perhaps he was abandoned, molested, abused, ridiculed, criticized, or told that he would never amount to anything.

The addict's early relationship with his parents has a lot to do with this particular core belief. A child gets his self-esteem from his parents; if the parent-child relationship is somehow dysfunctional, the child may view himself as worthless or defective.

In therapy, I must help clients see through this long-held cognitive distortion. They must see "I am bad" as a lie. I believe that the image of God is indelibly stamped in the soul of every person, giving each of us worth beyond measure. Thus, we are all fundamentally worthy of love, respect, and being valued.

2. *No one would love me as I am.*

This belief is another reflection of the addict's self-esteem. It is based largely on fear. The idea behind this one is, "I want to be loved and known intimately, but I am afraid that people who really got to know me would abandon me."

We are all afraid of rejection, and we are more afraid of being rejected by those who mean the most to us. The more we value another person, the more potential we have to be afraid of having that person know us. If one loses the friendship of an acquaintance, one has lost little. If one loses the friendship of one's life partner, one had lost much. To avoid such loss, we hide parts of our lives from others. We want others to be proud of us; we want them to think well of us. We want so badly to be loved and accepted by those who are important to us, yet we are afraid to reveal ourselves to them for fear of losing them.

In therapy, we are encouraged to be honest about ourselves, our past, and the struggles that we face. As we share honestly, we learn that people accept us regardless of what we have done or how we think or feel. As others accept us, we learn that we are acceptable, and we can begin to break down this lie.

My own experience was exactly this. I was afraid of telling anyone about my addiction, and yet I could not contain it anymore. I thought I didn't have any friends. I thought people liked me because of what I could do for them. However, as I looked at the people in my life, I found that I could build deeper relationships with them. I don't know how I did this. I think I simply exposed more and more of myself to a select group of people, and as my trust in them grew, I found that I could share more of myself.

3. *My needs are never going to be met if I have to depend on other people.*

Somewhere along the line, all addicts have been taught that our needs would not be met. Human beings have many different kinds of needs: emotional, physical, intellectual, spiritual, and sexual. At some point, though, those of us who have become addicts learned that we could not trust our parents or our friends to meet those needs.

With this in mind, you can see how a person would come to start relying on his own methods for meeting those needs. Children are taught by their parents how to meet their needs, but if parents are sick or the children are never taught, how do we learn to meet our needs? Children survive and cope as best they can, often by becoming self-reliant.

But just because our parents could not or would not meet our needs does not mean that our needs will never be met by others. To grow into healthy adults, we have to learn that others can be trusted to meet our needs.

It takes a great deal of courage to work through this. After all, we're not talking about needs like "I need a hamburger," but deep relational needs like "I need to know that I'm valuable to someone just for being myself." Group therapy and twelve-step support groups are a wonderful place to learn how to get those needs met.

4. *Sex is my most important need.*

I can hear the question, "How in the world can a person believe that sex is the most important need?" Often, this isn't a conscious belief, but often an unconscious one that is reflected in the addict's behavior.

Consider that an addict will take money that was destined for rent and use it to pay for a prostitute. An addict will skip work to meet a lover.

When a fix is needed, nothing else is allowed to get in the way. Health, job, family, relationships, and everything else gets pushed to the side.

So how do addicts overcome this lie that sex is our greatest need? We have to learn what the real need is and learn how to meet that need in a healthy way. In my experience, I would try to use sex to salve the emotions I was feeling. When I learned to deal with the emotions in a healthy way, the fix of sex was no longer necessary.

The Asian Double Bind

For Asians who are suffering in silence, this can create a double bind. They may want help. But how can they obtain it if it's viewed as being culturally reprehensible? Being out of control and needing emotional help is unacceptable to most Asians. But if they don't get help, they risk drowning in a sea of hopelessness that traps addicts and keeps them tumbling endlessly down this spiral of shame.

Traditional Asian parents can't tolerate a child's differences in thought and behavior because these differences cause too much distress in the parents. It is easier for them to assert their control over the child. When this happens, the child's thoughts and behaviors become repressed, and anxiety is created. The child never learns to connect to his parents with his real self. I see addictions as an unsuccessful but desperate attempt to reconnect with the true emotional aspects of an addict's self that were cut off years ago.

To feel excited but not to be able to show it, to feel like smiling but to be unable to smile, to feel like crying but to be unable to cry, to feel enraged but to swallow it, to feel terrified but to have to hide it, to feel ashamed but have to pretend that all is well, to feel disgust but have to smile—any and all of these are punitive experiences which produce affect hunger, the wish to express openly the incompletely suppressed affects. Alcohol has for centuries provided therapy for affect hunger of all kinds, releasing the smile of intimacy and tenderness, the look of excitement, sexual and otherwise, the unashamed crying of distress, the explosion of hostility, the intrusion of long-suppressed terror, the open confession of shame, and the avowal of self-contempt.

The shame that encompasses a person caught in addictions is really a soul crying out to be heard, understood, validated, and known. This was my shame.

Chapter 7
Shame And Sexuality

SHAME COMMUNICATES THE MESSAGE that we're weak, defective, dirty, and worthless. At a young age, Asians are taught to be strong and not show any weakness. So feelings of weakness or need in Asian cultures can trigger intense feelings of shame.

From an addict's perspective, it's the ultimate humiliation to be weak. After years of seeming self-sufficiency, the addict's acknowledgment that something else controls his life is demoralizing. It's difficult to admit to ourselves, our families, and our loved ones that we are need someone else's help, that we can't recover on our own. Yet it's this acknowledgment that prepares us for the road of recovery. In twelve-step meetings, it's known as "Step 1," when we break our excuses, rationalizations, and denial by acknowledging our powerlessness over our addiction.

The First Step Of Recovery

This first step is vital to recovery and is considered the most challenging because it forces addicts to break our own denial of the power of our addictions. We come to a point of brokenness where we realize we cannot control everything in our lives and must surrender that control to God. I think this is especially difficult for sexual addicts, since the addiction involves sexuality.

No other area is more misunderstood or shame-bound than the realm of sexuality. Our sexuality strikes at the core of who we are and cannot be cut off. Yet tension and shame arise when you are trapped in sexual obsessions or compulsions. "Just control your hormones" is the common exhortation. There's also the religious admonition to "Let go, and let God." Unfortunately this rhetoric leaves the struggling addict sinking even deeper into the pit of shame. Misunderstanding from well-meaning people only fuels feelings of defectiveness. The addict feels humiliated for not being able to keep his sexual desires and impulses in check.

Feeling flawed for having a sexual issue keeps the addict caught in a cycle of shame because sex and addiction conjure up images of dirtiness. Many of us grew up in homes where sex was never discussed. It was forbidden. If you did hear anything about sex, it was usually in church or a religious context, where you were given fair warning that God hates sexual immorality. Sexuality is presented as abhorrent unless it's confined to a loving, harmonious, marital relationship. You can see how this creates a shame-filled trap for those struggling with their sexual urges.

Any teenager or young adult may experience this link between shame and sexuality amid their newfound hormonal and sexual development. Feelings of fascination, excitement, and fear may crop up. However, if young people are in an oppressive Asian cultural or church context where space is not made to talk about sex or the struggles that come with abiding by God's unique design for intimacy, then shame is even more likely to set in. Asian young people often see themselves as "dirty" because of their sexuality.

Now imagine the heavy cloak of shame covering men and women who are caught in a web of sexual affairs, obsessions, and addictions. Whether it's a one-night stand, multiple affairs, visits to strip clubs, looking at porn, or compulsive masturbation, the combined feelings of dirtiness, defectiveness, and weakness all race to the forefront. When shame ensnares a person's entire core, he believes on an intrinsic level that he is unlovable, worthless, and a failure.

Chapter 8
Masculinity And Shame

WHAT DOES IT MEAN to be a man? This was a question that burned within me as a boy struggling to find the answer. In an Asian culture in which boys are shamed for having emotions and for caring, what was I to do with my emotions? Is it even "manly" to have them? What about my desire to have a deep connection with my parents and those around me? If not nurtured, a boy will walk a desolate emotional road, disconnected from his core.

As humans, we have a fundamental need to be in relationship with each other. You might be single, divorced, or living on a ranch in the wilderness, but our souls cannot thrive without relationship to our fellow man. We need emotional support. It can come from a family, a spouse, friends, or colleagues. It can happen at home, at work, at church, at a gym, or at school. But regardless of who or where it comes from, the desire and the demand for relationship never ceases in our lifetime.

However, images and clichés of "the self-made man," "rugged individualism," and "pulling yourself up by your bootstraps" counter this notion of group support. The Marlboro man was the image I remember as a kid, the cool, masculine, strong American cowboy who portrayed the epitome of individualism.

At the time, Marlboro was not a popular cigarette. Camel was leading the way. But the Marlboro Man portrayal of masculinity propelled Marlboro to the number one cigarette in the world, and the company has maintained that distinction for nearly thirty years.

This image of the rugged cowboy tackling life on his own became the measure of manhood. We must do "life" by ourselves. We should not depend on others for support or encouragement.

In an Asian American immigrant household, rugged self-reliance is even more prominent because parents may lack either the English verbal skills or willingness to connect with their children. If parents do not connect with their children on an emotional level and recognize their children's worth as distinct individuals, the kids grow up thinking they are not valued, hence creating shame.

> "The evolving bond between child and parent must be genuinely desired, expressed in word, and action, and also lived out consistently over time … This is an experience of being in relationship to another significant individual; it communicates that one is special to the other … When a child consistently fails to experience this distinct, individualized relationship, shame is generated because the interpersonal bridge is ruptured. The impact of parental actions *convinces* the child that he or she either counts as a person or instead is not wanted. (Kaufman 1996, 65-66)

In our family, the message repeated by our parents was to "get good grades, get a good job, get married, and have kids." I never felt they cared about my own heart's desires. There was never any attunement to my life, my hopes, or my dreams. I wanted my parents to ask about my school day, my favorite subjects, and other interests. Instead they operated with a hands-off approach to parenting that eventually left me with a gnawing sense of emptiness. I believed I was not worth much in their eyes.

To compound this emotional abandonment was the lack of affirming physical touch. There were no hugs or kisses—Asian kids were just supposed to know their parents loved them without any verbal or physical reminders of that love.

Multiple studies show that babies who are held, hugged, and kissed develop a healthier emotional life than those deprived of physical contact. My mom told me, "We love from our heart and that's what counts." However, without enough physical affirmation, serious relational ruptures occur. Children crave touch. They crave the opportunity to be held closely by their parents. Touch helps children feel safe, loved, and secure.

I remember my mom used to pick my earwax using a metal Chinese instrument. I savored every moment of having my ear on her lap. Whenever she was done and said she had found all the wax, I would always tell her to keep looking. I knew there wasn't much more wax to be excavated, but I yearned for a few more minutes of touch with Mom.

In fact, it wasn't until I was twenty-seven years old that I remember any more meaningful touch from her. At my wedding ceremony, I hugged my mom for the first time in my life. Tears inexplicably erupted and streaked down my face. I thought I was just caught up in the moment, but after reflection years later, I learned the tears symbolized a lifetime of sadness—the sadness and pain of never being allowed to be close to her.

When Asian parents do not express any verbal or physical signs of affection, their children lose any concrete sense of being loved unconditionally. Kaufman observes that "Physical touching is one of the principal ways of expressing affection or tenderness ... Hurting oneself, crying in distress, and then requiring physical contact with a parent is a typically observed pattern ... Holding communicates protection and security-the basis for trust" (Kaufman 1996 67). If the basis for trust is not established through hugs or physical touch during moments of physical trauma, then the child internalizes the emotion of shame for wanting to be touched by the parent.

> When the need for holding fails to be understood, however it happens, shame is generated. The child feels that either the self is deficient or the need is fundamentally bad. The need for holding becomes bound and eventually controlled by shame. (Kaufman 1996, 68).

But there are other aspects of our physical lives that must be shared with our parents. Questions about changes in our bodies that make us afraid or ashamed should be expressed.

In middle school, I noticed I had a severe rash on my arm that made it itchy. I would scratch it, and it would bleed. I didn't tell anyone about this because I was scared. Instead I tried to hide it. I remember my fear that classmates would tease me about this rash drove me to wear a jacket to cover it up, even during hot, sunny days. I also carried a bottle of lotion with me. I was embarrassed about ever letting anyone see my lotion or my rash. I didn't want to bother my parents and felt I was becoming a "problem" to them for even having this rash.

One of my first memories of being bullied was in elementary school. I belonged to an after-school track team with a friend from the neighborhood. Every day after school it was the same old drill: walk to the field and go to practice. However, on one of these days, another friend also came along, and the two of them took me aside and hit me hard for no reason. I started crying. I felt betrayed. I thought they were my friends. The lesson here is I was once again scared to tell my parents.

Since I hear story after story in therapy from clients who've had similar experiences, my hope is parents can pay better attention to their children. Much of a child's life can go undetected. If their lives are neglected, children learn they must take care of themselves because no one else will care for them. All of these separate incidents are small building blocks in developing a shame-based core.

When children are distressed, afraid, sad, hurt, or disappointed, these emotions need to be processed. Otherwise, shame begins its pernicious stranglehold on our souls.

Chapter 9
Shame And Childhood
"Asians Don't Cry"

GROWING UP IN AN immigrant Chinese household, the cultural values of harmony, collectivism, and family were embedded in our way of living. Emotionally, we were not encouraged to show any weakness. Strength and a strong will prevailed.

During my childhood, I don't recall ever having a conversation or being able to tell my parents when I felt anxious, scared, confused, angry, disappointed, or hurt. What was unconsciously ingrained in me was that it was not permissible to hurt, so when I did hurt, I just buried those feelings. By the time of my divorce, I knew it was socially acceptable to cry, yet the armor of repression was strong. The feelings had a hard time surfacing, at least until I was confronted.

The Power Of Group Therapy

During this period, I was participating in both individual counseling and group therapy. While I was gaining insight, I was not able to reach my emotional core until one night in group therapy, when the power of the group was unleashed. After nearly three months in the men's group therapy, the entire group confronted me as being "fake" and not being genuine with my emotions.

I wasn't moved at first. I simply responded, "I'm an optimist and don't need to dwell on being sad like you guys." However, the truth of the matter was that my soul never hurt more than it did that night. The stark reality of being in pain but not knowing how to release it led to what I consider my first honest prayer with God. Up to that point, I had made many "fortune cookie" prayers—prayers for more wealth, fame, possessions, and other selfish desires. This prayer was different. It was a guttural cry from the heart for God to dislodge the pain in my soul. God answered that prayer.

Through time and a commitment to the group therapy process, I received reassurance from the group that it was okay to weep and grieve. The pain, hurt, and feelings of abandonment erupted from the deepest cavity of my heart. I no longer had to live life putting on a fake exterior of being upbeat, entertaining, or fun. The façade I had worked so hard to develop in childhood would come down. I recorded this process in my journal.

Feb. 2003
God I am sorry for all the wrongs and hurts I've cause my wife, family, and close friends. I'm not asking for the pain to go away but I wish she could see I care about our relationship but am so tired and frustrated she won't communicate with me. I really wish I knew what my heart is feeling right now. It's so protected, I won't let anyone near it, including myself.

March 2003
The past few days have been quite a break-through. I'm beginning to allow my emotions and sadness to come out. In therapy I used four kleenexes! Very sad about losing her and my mother-in-law. I feel very lonely. They were the two people in the whole world I felt most connected to. Work-wise, I'm still unemployed but thinking about where God wants to use me.

After three years of counseling, I not only learned to grieve the adult loss of my marriage but also the unspoken disappointments of childhood in an Asian home. Some of those childhood wounds that were never talked about finally came up in my counseling sessions as I delved into the discovery of own deep-seated shame.

March 2003
I've been admiring how great it must feel to be a father close to his son. I've seen it with my martial arts instructor and his son. All the

while, I'm also feeling the pain of not having dad close to me and how hurt and fragile I am, even to this day. I am sad for him as well that grandpa didn't learn how to love his kids. I am now finally entering the grief stage.

I also went through a transformation or paradigm shift in terms of how I viewed people. In the past, I had judged others by their jobs or successes without learning to embrace a person simply as a child of God. I began to see people as human "beings" rather than human "doers."

April 2003

I am starting to see how desperately I've looked my whole life to find value in myself, value in my work to make me feel good about myself. That can't go on any longer. Sure I can have big dreams and go after success but I can't put my hope that success will fill me spiritually and emotionally.

I need to love myself right now for who I am, stripped of all things I've had that made me feel good. Job, wife, money, etc. I am a worthy person. A God-given gift to the world. I, you need to believe that!

May 2003

I praise God that two weeks ago with no money left and no job, I put my trust in God and he delivered! I was given an opportunity to work at a restaurant.

Sure I was just hosting. Sure it paid only $8.50/hr. Sure I made more in one hour in t.v. news than I did in an entire night's work there. Sure it was a bit humbling and discouraging. Sure it didn't look good on the resume. Sure it looked like I was settling for less. Yes, yes, yes, it was all these things and more.

But there was an invaluable lesson that I learned here, that I could not have received at a more "respectable" position—that even at the lowest career point in my life I still was surrounded by God's love. Believers were proud of me to do a noble thing (pay bills). Pastor Ken was excited for me, maybe because it gave me another place to share the fruits of the Spirit. Yes, what I didn't want to happen, happened. I looked at my life-long fear of failure squarely in the eye and knocked that foundation to the ground. It no longer will rule my life. Fear of failure is being replaced by the fear and grace of God.

But despite periods of epiphany, the process of growth is not always linear and positive. As you can see, there were many moments of doubt, despair, and setbacks.

August 2003
I feel terrible. Suffering from a hangover. Went to a club last night and got drunk, threw up, and missed church because of it. I also have been acting out a lot. Not sure why except maybe I'm feeling sad. My heart yearns to work but my spirit is losing hope.

Nevertheless, this period brought much restoration as I unearthed and processed my locked emotions. As I struggled to be real with my emotions, I wondered about the countless other Asian boys and girls.

Asian Parents And Emotions

Shame leaves one of its most damaging marks on children when parents expect and demand that their children keep emotions silent. When kids internalize that their parents will not be there for them emotionally, the message transmitted unwittingly is that "He or she is never to need anything emotionally from the parent; this communicates that the child should have been born an adult and therefore must relinquish childhood without ever having had it" (Kaufman 1996, 66). Shame naturally develops from this rupture. Children are taught that emotions are "bad" and they shouldn't need their parents to help them with their emotions.

Some parents cannot make an imaginative leap into a child's life, cannot tolerate a child's upset, cannot keep it straight that "parent" and "child" are two different minds and sensibilities, rather than one wise adult and one little, unformed mind needing control. Such parents often respond with trite, patronizing comments: "It's okay." "Don't worry." "It doesn't matter." But saying "It's all right" is one of the worst things parents can communicate to their kids, since it invalidates the child's own thoughts and feelings.

> "It's all right" is one of the biggest lies parents tell. Everything is "all right" if hurt isn't real, if the child's feelings don't count, if it doesn't matter that you shamed her or that Melissa said she was stupid. The misstatements of consolation are lies that seal away hurt as effectively as sweeping dirt under the carpet. If a parent, in his or her pride, does not allow a child to suffer, then a little pocket of suffering will be sealed away in memory, unexamined, unresponded to, unhealed. (Nichols 1991, 213)

When parents are inaccessible to their children physically and emotionally, the children feel abandoned and learn to keep their distance. Trust and relational dependence, core issues that promote intimacy, are then ruptured.

> "This produces a loss of trust and faith in relationships. Children feel that they are on their own, that people are unreliable and will eventually let them down, lose interest, or turn away" (Dayton 2000, 62).

Author and counselor John Bradshaw eloquently put it best when he defined what it means to live in a shame-filled body:

> To be shame-bound means that whenever you feel any feeling, need or drive, you immediately feel ashamed. The dynamic core of your human life is grounded in your feelings, needs and drives. When these are bound by shame, you are shamed to the core. (Bradshaw 1988, 32)

My First Memory: Abandonment

In *The Road Less Traveled*, M. Scott Peck (1978) asks readers to think of their first recollection of life. This memory, he believes, can give you great depth of insight into your motivations and general outlook on life.

For myself, my first distinct memory is of terror. I was stuck on a merry-go-round as my mother was walking away. In hindsight, she may have just stepped a few feet away, possibly trying to empower me to leave on my own accord yet I was paralyzed in fear. The sight left me in a state of panic. I came to see her as unsafe.

This was made evident when I hurt myself after I fell while playing basketball. The side of my leg bled profusely. I was scared and didn't know where to go. Instead of returning home and possibly upsetting or disappointing my mother, I went to my grandmother's house located a couple blocks from my parents' house. My grandmother was very disturbed that I was so afraid to go home.

Later in therapy, we processed how I internalized that my mom would be displeased and not want me.

June 2003

I cried so hard in therapy my eyes still hurt (11 hours later). We touched on some very raw feelings today regarding my perception of myself. I have learned in the past that I could never hurt physically and ever since then it translated into trying to never get hurt emotionally.

I get so scared of being rejected and not accepted by others that it's hard for me to allow others to see that I'm vulnerable as opposed to being all-knowing. I don't ever want someone to think I'm inadequate or uninformed so I've done a lot of hiding.

When I was ten years old, the indelible mark of childhood abandonment was seared on my heart after a terrifying experience during the summer. During those long days, with no money or organized activities as resources, we would meet other kids in the neighborhood and use our creativity to play. Sometimes we caught bees in Mason jars; other times we made mud-balls in my grandmother's backyard.

On this occasion, we found some used car tires and decided to have a contest. The goal was to see who could roll his tire the farthest down the hill. To my surprise, while the other tires bobbled and collapsed in the middle of the road, my tire kept rolling. It rolled so far that it hit a parked car at the bottom of the street. All the other kids, sensing danger, quickly scattered. I, on the other hand, didn't know better. I walked down to the house where the car was parked and knocked on the door to claim responsibility. The owner came out and asked me to take him to my parents.

When I arrived home and explained to my mom in Chinese what had happened, the owner told my mom she would have to reimburse him for the damages. My mom said she couldn't afford it and offered me instead. At first I was confused. Then she started pushing me toward him and yelling in broken English, "Take him, take him!"

Panic pierced my soul. I remember kicking, crying, and screaming. The guy got spooked and left. I walked back through the front door like a dog with his tail between his legs. I was shocked, hurt, angry, and confused by the emotional storm I had just weathered.

My mother offered no words of comfort, so I harbored this traumatizing experience internally. The sense of betrayal and fear of abandonment was complete. I never wanted to experience this again. I hated feeling so alone and unwanted.

How could I feel "wanted" by others? True to my Asian culture, I tried to feel wanted by becoming a good student, but I wasn't that great. I tried to be a good basketball player, but there were always better ones. What could I do to feel treasured?

Now looking back, I can see how these experiences and thoughts were unconsciously sowing the seeds of my addiction, which was rooted in a distorted belief that I was not wanted or worthy of love.

Chapter 10
The Making Of Asian Addiction

IN THERAPY, WE LOOK for patterns: individual patterns and family ones. What is striking is the patterns that emerge from addicted families. Research shows addicts come from families in which there's a prevalence of rigid and disengaged family interactions.

In what's known as the circumplex model of family systems, we can see how different levels of cohesion, flexibility, and communication produce certain patterns in families that can make a family member more susceptible to addictions compared to people from different family systems.

The major hypothesis of the circumplex model is that balanced family systems tended to be more functional than unbalanced systems.

Family Cohesion (Togetherness)

Family cohesion is defined *as the emotional bonding that family members have toward one another.* Within the circumplex model, some of the specific concepts or variables that can be used to diagnose and measure family cohesion are emotional bonding, boundaries, coalitions, time, space, friends, decision-making, and interests and recreation. The focus of cohesion is how systems balance their separateness versus togetherness.

There are four levels of cohesion, ranging from *disengaged* (very low) to *separated* (low to moderate) to *connected* (moderate to high) to *enmeshed* (very high) (See diagram).

Circumplex Model of Marital & Family Systems

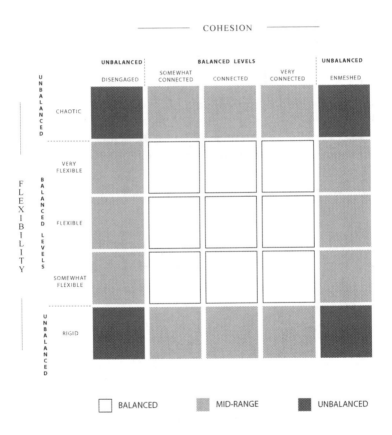

The central or balanced levels of cohesion (separated and connected) make for optimal family functioning. The extreme or unbalanced levels (disengaged and enmeshed) are generally seen as problematic for relationships over the long term.

In the model's balanced area of cohesion (separated and connected), individuals are able to experience and balance these two extremes and are also able to be both independent from and connected to their families. Many families that go for therapy often fall into one of the extreme or unbalanced areas. When cohesion levels are very high (enmeshed systems), there is too much consensus within the family and limited independence or individuation. At the other extreme (disengaged systems), family members "do their own thing," with limited attachment or commitment to their family. (Olson 2006)

When it comes to disengaged families, there is little trust or desire to share stories, hopes and dreams, fears and concerns, and the emotional or interior world with each other. Family members feel like they are "ships passing in the night." Conversations stay superficial and safe. Very rarely are there heart-to-heart talks; fear is too high in these families.

This disengaged style is the pattern I grew up in. My hopes, dreams, and concerns could not be brought to light as I feared being ridiculed or shamed. Attachment with my parents or brothers is hard. Intimacy is not what we are accustomed to. Conversations with Dad are limited to clichés about "working hard," "staying out of trouble," and being a "good son."

With my mother, it's better now. We can talk more about my work situation and my concerns with finances. Still, due to both cultural and intimacy issues, our conversations are restricted to staying upbeat about life, with the occasional financial lecture.

I remember a conversation with her regarding my training in counseling as sex addiction therapist and how it would cost eight thousand dollars to complete. She just sighed and commented that it sounded like a waste of money. She could not understand how, despite the cost, some things are necessary. I told her this was an investment in my training and would pay off later, but these concepts are difficult for my parents to understand. The notion of graduate school and taking out student loans seems ludicrous to them.

My brothers avoid anything relational. This means talking about concerns we have with each other or about their lives is off-limits. When I challenge them and break the family rules, I'm often met with passivity. My brothers do not want to talk about our issues—they hope any problem will just subside if they ignore the subject.

In Asian families that are disengaged, there is limited emotional investment in each other's lives. Without an emotional investment, there will be ruptured attachment or bonding between family members. The unspoken rule is to stay independent of each other for fear of any need to rely on each other for support or help. Emotional dependence on anyone within the family may bring up feelings of defectiveness and shame, since the individual's overwhelming desire in this system is for emotional independence. Anything less might be interpreted as being "needy" and thus shameful.

A *disengaged relationship* is often marked by extreme emotional separateness. Individuals often do their own thing; separate time, space, and interests predominate; and members are unable to turn to one another for support and problem-solving. Research shows 88% of addicts come from disengaged families. (Carnes 1991)

Family Flexibility

Rigidity refers to the limited negotiation that is possible regarding roles and rules within the household.

The four levels of flexibility range from *rigid* (very low) to *structured* (low to moderate) to *flexible* (moderate to high) to *chaotic* (very high) (See Figure 1). As with cohesion, it is hypothesized that central or balanced levels of flexibility (structured and flexible) are more conducive to good marital and family functioning, with the extremes (rigid and chaotic) being the most problematic for families as they move through their life cycles.

Balanced family systems (structured and flexible types) tend to be more functional over time. A *structured relationship* tends to have a somewhat democratic leadership, with some negotiations including the children. Roles are stable with some sharing of roles. There are few rule changes with rules firmly enforced.

A *flexible relationship* has equalitarian leadership with a democratic approach to decision-making. Negotiations are open and actively include the children. Roles are shared, and there is fluid change when necessary. Rules can be changed and are age appropriate.

Unbalanced families tend to be either rigid or chaotic. A *rigid relationship* is characterized by one individual being in charge and highly controlling. Negotiations are limited, with most decisions imposed by the leader. Roles are strictly defined and the rules do not change. A *chaotic relationship*, by contrast, has erratic or limited leadership. Decisions are impulsive and not well thought out. Roles are unclear and often shift from individual to individual.

Very high levels of flexibility (chaotic) and very low levels of flexibility (rigid) tend to be problematic for individuals and relationship development in the long run. On the other hand, relationships having moderate scores (structured and flexible) are able to balance change and stability in a more functional way. (Olson 2006)

When it comes to Asian families, rigidity in which parents are always right is often in play. Children have little voice to make decisions or negotiate changes. This is significant for addicts. An addict from a rigid Asian family has learned as a core value that he has no "voice" to impact relationships, and thus must turn elsewhere to get his relational needs met. He must find another place where he can have influence, and thus turns to addiction.

Within relationships, addicts learn they cannot trust that their voices have impact, and thus they must remain silent. The interior monologue of an addict goes something like this: "Why bother to tell someone what I feel, since it won't change anything anyway?"

I kept any conflict off the table in my romantic relationships, especially my marriage. Why bring up an issue, since I would have no impact on the outcome? Major decisions such as children, where to go on vacations, and how money would be invested or spent were left to my wife. I felt I had no right to express an opinion.

By failing to participate, I also slowly gave away a part of my soul. During my counseling sessions, I realized small issues such as my taste in music had also been compromised because of my fear that my wife and her family would abandon me.

Journal Entry, July 2003

In therapy, Dr. Simpson felt I'm doing something significant in re-claiming a lost part of me in the form of r&b songs. The must that I felt was so much a part of my identity was repressed during marriage and work.

I was ashamed for liking that kind of music. My in-laws would put it down, calling it "un-classy". I wouldn't tell people at work that I loved r&b because I didn't want them to think "less" of me. It even got so bad, that I gave away more than 100 cds, thinking I would sacrifice this music altogether to "prove" to Susan I had changed into a man of God. But now I've learned being a man of God is being honest to myself."

Life is about setting boundaries, and in my desire to be liked by my wife and colleagues, I had tried to mirror their desires and wishes. In essence, I had poor boundaries and lost all sense of who I was as a person.

Shame And Boundaries

Shame-based relationships lack good boundaries when it comes to communication. In a dynamic and healthy relationship, boundaries give us a sense of where we are and where another person begins. Think of a fence between two homeowners. The fence is a physical boundary that gives both owners a clear, visible demarcation between one person's property and that of his neighbor.

In unhealthy relationships, the boundaries are either too loose or too rigid. In those with rigid boundaries, a defensive wall is erected for protection and prevents intimacy. The internalized belief process of a person with rigid boundaries goes something like this: "No one can see me, and I can't see others." Intimacy is limited because everyone is kept at an arm's length. Loving, caring, listening, nurturing, guiding, teaching, and modeling are not taking place. Children feel their parents don't love them because they are lonely. These children are not able to talk to their parents, since they've learned their parents won't listen to them (Laaser 1992). Without communication, a wall begins to form, and no one is allowed "in". This can lead to crippling feelings of abandonment and worthlessness.

At the other extreme are relationships marked by extremely loose boundaries that a person cannot ask another to respect. Basically personal space is being violated in these relationships. Imagine a weak fence that allows your neighbor to walk into your yard without your permission. When boundaries are too loose, you have no protection. When others invade your boundaries (i.e. go too far physically or emotionally) and you can't say no, then you have loose boundaries. When you are hit, yelled at, sexually touched, or preached at inappropriately and feel you don't have control over your own body, mind, emotions, or spirit, you end up letting abuse happen to you (Laaser 1992).

In Asian families, problems with communication occur because children are often not allowed to articulate their own thoughts or not encouraged to speak up for themselves. These children grow up believing their thoughts and feelings don't count in relationships, since their thoughts and feelings were not allowed in their families. When such children enter romantic relationships, they stand a high percentage chance of dismissing not only their own thoughts and feelings but their partner's as well.

Attachment And Sex Addiction

People are perplexed when I tell them, "Sex addiction isn't about sex." Instead, it's about an inability to form healthy attachment bonds, an inability often developed during one's childhood. Sex addiction therapists describe it as an "intimacy disorder."

People generally fall into one of four attachment styles: *secure, anxious-preoccupied, dismissing-avoidant,* or *fearful avoidant.*

1. *Secure Attachment*

   People who have secure attachment are those who score low on anxiety and avoidance. They are comfortable being emotionally close to a partner and asking for help, and they do not fear being alone, without a partner. Research indicates securely attached people tend to agree with the following statements: "It is relatively easy for me to become emotionally close to others. I am comfortable depending on others and having others depend on me. I don't worry about being alone or having others not accept me" (Mikulincer and Shaver 2007)

2. *Anxious-Preoccupied Attachment*

This category describes people who are preoccupied with "losing a partner" and are consumed by thoughts of abandonment (whether real or perceived). An anxious-preoccupied person may become dependent and worry if his partner hasn't responded to him within an expected time frame after he has left text messages or voice mails. He may come off as "clingy" or "controlling" because of his need to be close to his partner. People who are anxious or preoccupied with attachment tend to agree with the following statements: "I want to be completely emotionally intimate with others, but I often find that others are reluctant to get as close as I would like. I am uncomfortable being without close relationships, but I sometimes worry that others don't value me as much as I value them" (Mikulincer and Shaver 2007).

3. *Dismissing Attachment*

People with this style are very disengaged and "dismiss" their need for relationships despite being in them. They desire a high level of independence, which often appears as an attempt to avoid attachment altogether. They view themselves as self-sufficient and invulnerable to the feelings associated with being closely attached to others. They often deny needing close relationships. Some may even view close relationships as relatively unimportant. People with a dismissive attachment style tend to suppress and hide their feelings, and they often deal with rejection by distancing themselves from the sources of rejection (i.e. their relationship partners). They tend to agree with these statements: "I am comfortable without close emotional relationships. It is very important to me to feel independent and self-sufficient, and I prefer not to depend on others or have others depend on me" (Mikulincer and Shaver 2007).

4. *Fearful-Avoidant Attachment*

People with this attachment style have mixed feelings about close relationships. On the one hand, they desire to have emotionally close relationships. On the other hand, they tend to feel uncomfortable with emotional closeness. These mixed feelings are combined with negative views about themselves and their partners. They commonly view themselves as unworthy of responsiveness from their partners, and they don't trust the intentions of their partners. People with a fearful–avoidant attachment style seek less intimacy from partners and frequently hide their feelings. They tend to agree with the following statements: "I am uncomfortable getting close to others. I want emotionally close relationships, but I find it difficult to trust others completely, or to depend on them. I worry that I will be hurt if I allow myself to become too close to others" (Mikulincer and Shaver 2007).

Avoidant Attachment and Sexual Addiction

Most addicts have what therapists call an attachment or intimacy disorder. Addicts have never learned how to trust, become dependent on others for help, and build connectedness. Consequently, they have been shown to develop "templates," or routines of thought and behavior, that make them more vulnerable to sexual addiction.

[A]dolescents and young adults who scored higher on avoidance were more interested in emotionless sex, were less likely to be involved in sexually exclusive relationships, and were more likely to have sex with a stranger and engage in "one night stands." (Bogaert, A. F. and Sadava, S. (2002)

So how does an avoidant attachment style promote addiction? Since avoidants are emotionally dismissive or anxious, they are uncomfortable with being close to someone emotionally. The discomfort with closeness gives them the cognitive ability to compartmentalize sex as separate from a relationship.

> Avoidant people may be willing to engage in sex without any consideration of establishing a long-term relationship, or even with the conviction that they do not want to be burdened by a long-term relationship. In other words, avoidance may be associated with erotophobia (fear or backing away from sex), sexual abstinence, or preference for impersonal, uncommitted sex. (Mikulincer & Shaver 2007, 351)

In contrast, those with secure attachments believe they can find romantic love based on intimacy and vulnerability within a committed relationship.

If you are wondering what your attachment style is, please look through these statements to gauge your own comfort level with closeness. Items 1–18 measure a person's anxiety, whereas items 19–36 measure level of avoidance.

1. *I'm afraid that I will lose my partner's love.*
2. *I often worry that my partner will not want to stay with me.*
3. *I often worry that my partner doesn't really love me.*
4. *I worry that romantic partners won't care about me as much as I care about them.*
5. *I often wish that my partner's feelings for me were as strong as my feelings for him or her.*
6. *I worry a lot about my relationships.*
7. *When my partner is out of sight, I worry that he or she might become interested in someone else.*
8. *When I show my feelings for romantic partners, I'm afraid they will not feel the same about me.*

9. *I rarely worry about my partner leaving me.*
10. *My romantic partner makes me doubt myself.*
11. *I do not often worry about being abandoned.*
12. *I find that my partner(s) don't want to get as close as I would like.*
13. *Sometimes romantic partners change their feelings about me for no apparent reason.*
14. *My desire to be very close sometimes scares people away.*
15. *I'm afraid that once a romantic partner gets to know me, he or she won't like who I really am.*
16. *It makes me mad that I don't get the affection and support I need from my partner.*
17. *I worry that I won't measure up to other people.*
18. *My partner only seems to notice me when I'm angry.*
19. *I prefer not to show a partner how I feel deep down.*
20. *I feel comfortable sharing my private thoughts and feelings with my partner.*
21. *I find it difficult to allow myself to depend on romantic partners.*
22. *I am very comfortable being close to romantic partners.*
23. *I don't feel comfortable opening up to romantic partners.*
24. *I prefer not to be too close to romantic partners.*
25. *I get uncomfortable when a romantic partner wants to be very close.*
26. *I find it relatively easy to get close to my partner.*
27. *It's not difficult for me to get close to my partner.*
28. *I usually discuss my problems and concerns with my partner.*
29. *It helps to turn to my romantic partner in times of need.*
30. *I tell my partner just about everything.*
31. *I talk things over with my partner.*
32. *I am nervous when partners get too close to me.*
33. *I feel comfortable depending on romantic partners.*
34. *I find it easy to depend on romantic partners.*
35. *It's easy for me to be affectionate with my partner.*
36. *My partner really understands me and my needs.*
    (Fraley, Waller, and Brennan 2000)

For a more exact analysis of your attachment style, you can participate in a free assessment at the Your Personality website, which hosts several questionnaires at www.yourpersonality.net. The relationship questionnaire (http://www.yourpersonality.net/cgi-bin/relationships/getsurvey.pl) is part of a study being conducted by the University of Illinois at Urbana-Champaign and is open to everyone.

Chapter 11
Asian Shame And Imperfection

ASKING FOR HELP IS hard to do. For an Asian person, it is often seen as the ultimate moral failure. "In China, for instance, addiction is still widely viewed as profound moral failing demanding punitive action. Many Chinese drug abusers are sent to labor camps, where they receive little treatment"(Denizet-Lewis 2009, 9).

We cannot help ourselves out of our hole, and yet by acknowledging our addiction to others, we would be considered shameful by our families and our Asian culture. We must either overcome our shame or potentially succumb to long-term, debilitating bouts with depression, suicide, and feelings of inadequacy.

My divorce forced me to ask for help, as the pain was too unbearable for me to shoulder alone. I was fortunate to be in a community where I was encouraged by those around me to seek help and support. Despite my growth, the tentacles of Asian shame still arise in my life as I strive for perfection in my recovery.

Having completed my master's degree in clinical psychology and invested more than four years in therapy, I still struggle. Why won't God just take this away? I think part of the reason is God wants me to remain humble. It would be easy to have an air of superiority and self-righteousness if I could stand before others and proclaim that I never experience sexual temptation anymore. Most Asian church circles would be much more comfortable if I was totally "healed" and "restored" by God's grace to the point that sexual struggles never came up again.

Mine is not that story. Mine is a story of messy spirituality in which I fall, repent, get back up, and try again. By this process, I come to truly rest on his "Amazing Grace."

> Therefore, in order to keep me from becoming conceited, I was given a thorn in my flesh, a messenger of Satan, to torment me. Three times I pleaded with the Lord to take it away from me. But he said to me, "My grace is sufficient for you, for my power is made perfect in weakness." Therefore I will boast all the more gladly about my weaknesses, so that Christ's power may rest on me. That is why, for Christ's sake, I delight in weaknesses, in insults, in hardships, in persecutions, in difficulties. For when I am weak, then I am strong. (2 Corinthians 12:7-10 TNIV)

Honestly, living in this tension is the most torturous aspect of life. It's easy to feel confident when you can tell the world, "I've been sober for five years." It's easy for a church or organization to ask you to speak when they consider you "successful" in your recovery. But that's living in a black-and-white world. How do I see myself when I'm not there yet? Can I still feel God's acceptance when I must deal with shades of gray? Is God's love still available to me? Can I tell myself it's okay being in the midst of my struggle, or do I berate myself for not living up to other people's standards? I yearn to soak in God's unfailing love and forgiveness and am reminded of it in the Serenity Prayer.

> *God grant me the serenity to accept the things*
> *I cannot change; courage to change the things I*
> *can; and wisdom to know the difference.*
>
> *-Reinhold Niebuhr*

Shame's Impact On Romance

Shame adversely affects our closest relationships. A shame-based person stands a good chance of being caught in a shame-based romantic relationship that mirrors his childhood pattern of dysfunction.

Shame-based relationships lack good boundaries. One clinical example is a client who had divorced three times because he felt "controlled and used." He had broken up with his latest girlfriend, but not before it became apparent he was allowing her to use him. He had agreed to pay her rent and pay for a live-in maid even though she was a wealthy businesswoman. He described it as a way to "win her love," but he later realized it was more a case of weak boundaries and a fear of abandonment. Had he expressed his feelings of not wanting to pay for those things early on, he risked her possibly leaving the relationship. In the end, the relationship collapsed anyway, as she did not respect his inability to draw healthy boundaries with himself and in his relationship with her.

With unresolved childhood shame, adults like this client are likely to enter romantic relationships desperately seeking approval— so much so that they'll lose themselves in their relationships to satisfy their partners. These folks will justify their behavior by saying that "Love is about compromise and sacrifice," yet they will refuse to acknowledge that they're sacrificing themselves, their ideals, and their souls to get the love they never got from their primary caregivers.

This dynamic is known as codependency. The need to win a spouse's approval and prevent abandonment is so strong that it chokes off the desire for true intimacy. I know this because I've lived this.

How I became a "Yes" Man

"Sure."

"No problem."

"Yeah, I can do that. Whatever you want."

"No worries."

"Walk over me? Fine."

"Hit me or beat me up? Let me turn the other cheek."

"Degrade me? Okay."

I don't know how it happened, but my desire for approval was so strong that I was unabashedly a "yes" man for much of my life. I didn't realize how strong my desire for approval was until I met the woman who would become my wife. After we had been dating a few months, she wanted to introduce me to her parents but forewarned me that they would disapprove of my parents' professional background. Her parents were well-educated, affluent, working professionals. Her father was an engineering professor at the University of Toledo, and her mother had a master's degree in education. My parents hadn't finished high school and were barely surviving financially. She asked me to lie about my parents' upbringing or at least be very vague.

So, without a question, that's what I did. I "obeyed" and mentioned that my dad was a "chef". I had felt shame about myself before, but this time it sank into the deepest recesses of my heart. I felt that the core of my being was inadequate. The inadequacy was not limited just to me, but included my parents, and by extension to my Chinese heritage. Everything I was, I interpreted as not being "good enough" for her. Even though it's been more than a decade since then, the hurt of having sacrificed so much of myself for her approval still echoes within my heart.

But that was just the beginning of my extreme effort to gain her approval. Before our marriage, she insisted that I would have to take her Korean name so I quickly agreed to drop my Chinese middle name and adopt her Korean name. In addition, I agreed that our children would carry her family name as a way to perpetuate her family's honor.

I agreed to all this without much fuss, thinking I was performing my marital duty of "sacrifice." It would have been fine if it was something I was okay with, but I later realized I acted out of fear. It was unhealthy to comply with her requests because I was afraid she'd leave me if I didn't.

Shortly after we got married, and I was still working in Ohio, she decided she wanted to move to New York City and pursue a career in acting. As a new husband, who was I to object? Shouldn't I be supportive of her interests? So, naturally, I agreed with her desire to find work as an actor even though I was uncomfortable with the thought of a long-distance relationship. Her brother-in-law asked me point-blank, "Sam, are you fine with this?"

I simply replied, "Yes, because this is what marriage is about—sacrifice!"

My wife left for New York while we were still newlyweds, and I remained in Ohio trying to support two rent payments on one salary. The long-distance relationship didn't last for more than a year before I was promoted to work in Los Angeles. It was a dream come true for the both of us. She could act, I could work in TV news, and we could live together! "Is God good or what?" I thought.

But nothing could have prepared us for life in Los Angeles. While it was glamorous to be working in television, it was also brutal. Co-workers would befriend me and betray me; people I met often wanted my friendship because of what I could "give" them through my connections and the community I was entrenched in was all about success, beauty, and superficiality.

Finances somehow became a subject of contention. It bewildered me, as I was making nearly six figures. My wife took care of all the finances, and when she would explain to me we were "losing" money every month, I felt hopeless. How could I be making what appeared to me to be a lot of money and still come up short? I just internalized the feeling of not being "good enough" all over again. Would I ever be "good enough" in her eyes?

On the spiritual front, I was so preoccupied with work that I never invested in our spiritual relationship. Sure, we went to church and even belonged to a small group comprised of young married couples, but as a Christian I was once again "not good enough." She often would ask to pray together, and I would just shrug my shoulders and do it halfheartedly. I guess it was difficult for someone like me, who was not used to prayer, to be asked to pray with her before going to bed as it triggered more feelings of spiritual shame and inferiority.

Eventually, we became like ships passing in the night. I worked a swing shift and she was usually asleep when I returned home. It didn't help that prior to work, I often played pickup basketball at the local YMCA , partially to avoid being at home with her. It was only a matter a time before she asked me to limit my basketball so we could spend "quality" time together. It's true, I probably gravitated to the basketball court as a way of avoiding having to deal with the fissures showing up in our relationship, but that was the only way I knew how to deal with issues.

Eventually she demanded that I stop basketball altogether and take up another hobby, possibly martial arts since she felt she wanted to feel more "protected." I was willing to oblige but knew nothing about martial arts. I searched for the most effective martial arts and came across Brazilian jiu-jitsu (BJJ). Unlike the popular sport it is today, in 2000 BJJ was a nascent martial art and seemed like a secret society made up of just a handful of us at our dojo in Hollywood. I was immediately hooked by it. I loved the physical contact, the camaraderie, and our instructor John Machado, whose family was considered the cousins of the well-known Gracies.

Despite my love of the sport, when my wife saw me during practice one night, she wanted me to stop. She didn't like the look of me wrestling with guys on the floor. I knew I was entering a new territory of shame when even my choice of martial arts was not good enough for her.

When it came to work, my wife watched me every night on the news and gave me constructive feedback. But it got to the point that she was uncomfortable with our sexually charged newscasts and wanted me to say something to my bosses. I was often sent to cover lingerie modeling shoots or the Playboy Mansion. It got so bad that a Latino guy in his twenties working at Rite-Aid once saw me in Westwood and exclaimed, "Hey, aren't you the Playboy reporter?" As if my personal life weren't bad enough, now the station I was working for and the assignments I was asked to do also weren't good enough for her.

Despite all these experiences with my ex-wife that indicate a lack of personal understanding of the difference between sacrifice for the sake of the other and the sacrifice of one's soul for approval, the experience that best encapsulates my inability to draw boundaries and say no was not with a woman but with a man.

Distant Dad

Before I go there, I must start by sharing a bit about my relationship with my father. I grew up with an Asian dad who was distant. He worked long hours in the kitchen to support our family, and when he was home, he had no time to invest in us kids. He could not speak English and I couldn't speak Chinese well enough to communicate with him. But besides that, there was also a cultural divide. What could my dad possibly understand about growing up in America since he was raised in Hong Kong? How were we to connect emotionally?

As a man, it hurts to not know your father. Other than his job as a chef, his taste for cheap beer (Pabst Blue Ribbon), or his time spent watching Chinese soap operas, I have no idea where his heart is. But I think the hurt cuts deeper knowing he has no idea where my heart is either. My cares, worries, desires, and longings in life could not be shared with him. It's a great psychic loss few Asians or men in general like to acknowledge for fear of appearing weak. It's also poor behavior to bash your parents, which is how some Asians have viewed my verbalization of parental disappointment.

Having lost my father's love and approval, What did exist was a Christian community made up of men whom I admired. One of them chose to mentor me for a couple of years during high school. Despite my incompetence as a student (flunking trigonometry), this man still invested time each week to help me study, teach me how to play the guitar, and care about my life.

I look back now and see this as precious. How and why would someone care so much about me? I wasn't related to him. He barely knew me. He didn't want anything from me. While he wanted me to do well in school, I felt he also was willing to just accept me where I was at.

This man was my first, true Christian mentor. A man who exemplified his faith by his investment in my life. A man who poured out God's love onto me. It's a love that I never forgot. It's partly why I am passionate about mentoring, especially in an age when so many boys grow up without fathers and in fragmented communities with limited access to older men.

My Mentor And Betrayal

Years later, I would meet a mentor who was someone I truly wanted to be like. He was smart, well-dressed, respected, and admired in television news. I met him at a journalism convention, and he took a liking to my passion and desire for storytelling. Over the course the next formative years in my career, he gave me professional advice, encouragement, and support.

I distinctly remember a time at a silent auction when he saw a book I wanted and decided to outbid everyone else by putting down a figure that was well over what the book was worth. When asked by a woman who wanted the book why he did that, he simply looked at me and said, "It's for Sam." That moment made me feel so cherished

A few years later, he was in charge of hiring for a news station in Los Angeles. He came across my résumé tape and decided to fly me to LA for an interview. He was not only my mentor but now would possibly also be my boss. Could this get any better? Well, after meeting the staff and seeing a full-blown newsroom in operation, I was spinning at the possibility of working in Los Angeles, considered the media capital of the world.

I met several other top managers and went to dinner with them. All the while I was wondering, "When's the interview?" Apparently, it was a done deal since he knew me, liked me, and wanted me there. No formal interview needed. The adage of "it's not what you know but who you know" was becoming a personal truth for me.

On my last night there, my mentor asked if I'd like to eat at Morton's Steakhouse, the famous location of the annual *Vanity Fair* Oscar party where the Hollywood elite gathered to celebrate. I was already awestruck by the pulse of Los Angeles; this would be the cherry on top before I returned to give my two weeks' notice to the station I worked for in Ohio.

I met my mentor at his place beforehand, since he would be driving us to the restaurant. When I arrived, he was already busy making the then-popular apple martini to start off the night. After the first one, he encouraged me to drink another, but I informed him of my "Asian flu" (many Asians lack the enzyme to digest alcohol), so off we went to Morton's.

Once inside, I was very impressed by the professionalism of the staff and their treatment of my mentor. He appeared to be a regular there. I still could not believe I was at the place where Hollywood celebrities mingled during the Oscars. Soon I would be working in the city of my dreams! My heart was pounding with exhilaration.

During our dinner, my mentor ordered wine to complement the meal and afterward finished with a dessert wine. By this time I was starting to feel a bit sick. We left and were driving back to my hotel when he asked if I'd like to check out a nightclub. Since I never experienced the "L.A. nightlife", I thought this was be a great opportunity. But as we approached the club, I noticed it was a gay bar and by then I felt obligated to keep my word. I noticed as he was guiding me through the club that he also began holding my hand. I was perplexed and allowed him to continue doing so for fear of reprisal.

A short time later, we left and he urged me to go back to his place for a drink. I told him I could not drink any more. He then gave me a look of disapproval and disappointment. Feeling pressured, I agreed but insisted on not drinking.

When we got inside, we sat down on his couch and he began rubbing my chest and kissing my neck. I remember feeling disgusted at myself that I couldn't protest and was allowing this to take place. I felt so violated yet he never forced himself on me. I had agreed to let him touch me. He also asked me to take off my pants, at which point I recoiled and left in horror.

A few hours later on an early morning flight back to Ohio, my entire system was in the throes of alcohol poisoning. I was stuck in the plane's bathroom trying to vomit out the alcohol, but nothing would come out because I was dehydrated. It was Christmas Eve, and I remember families being on the flight. Many passengers looked at me with derision. They clearly wondered why a grown man like myself was getting violently drunk on Christmas Eve for all to see.

Upon my arrival in Ohio I was a crumpled mess. My then wife and her family took me to the emergency room where I spent the next twenty-four hours hooked up to an IV and recovering from alcohol poisoning.

Afterward, I thought over the events in anguish. Had I been groomed all these years? Did he see me as just a sex toy? Was his desire to hire me genuine or just a ploy to get into my pants? I was horrified, embarrassed, and unable to answer questions from my in-laws. Why hadn't I just said no? Why had I gone along with it? Was I gay? My character seemed to be under attack.

Deep inside, I realized I had a problem, I never knew I had the right to say no. I did not see myself as someone who had a voice that mattered in this world.

I look back on this breach of trust and questioned my self-worth and competency in journalism. I always doubted I was "good enough" to work in Los Angeles as the reason for my hiring was muddied with sexual overtones.

I believe unequivocally that, like me, many addicts who grew up in families without proper gender nurturing have a cosmic vacuum within their souls that cannot be filled sexually. The central issue of a person's eternal purpose, glory, and relationship with his Creator may be obscured by his search for identity, community, trust, love, intimacy, and acceptance. These issues are a part of my own sexual struggle, so it's my belief that these issues also shared by others, straight or gay, who are grappling with questions of faith, sex, and God's unique design in creating us male or female.

Chapter 12

Asian Shame And Sex Addiction

2006 Worldwide Pornography Revenues
http://internet-filter-review.toptenreviews.com/internet-pornography-statistics.html

Country Revenue (in billions of US dollars)
1. *China $27.40*
2. *South Korea $25.73*
3. *Japan $19.98*
4. *US $13.33*
5. *Australia $2.00*
6. *UK $1.97*
7. *Italy $1.40*
8. *Canada $1.00*
9. *Philippines $1.00*
10. *Taiwan $1.00*

STATISTICS SHOW REVENUES DERIVED from pornography worldwide are highest among Asian countries. Out of the top 10 countries contributing to porn revenues, five of them are in Asia. Most telling is that China, South Korea, and Japan rank first, second, and third.

Based on my understanding of psychology, culture, and addiction, it's no surprise that Asians are most susceptible to misusing and abusing their sexuality. As we know, Asian societies base their identities and traditions on shame. Shame is what sets limits to our behavior and keeps us "in check." By being obedient and trying our best to put family first, we try not to disgrace our families and heritage. Our individuality is often suppressed, to the point that many Asians lack an individual sense of self because of their need for parental and cultural approval.

But the old way of thinking is being reworked, especially here in America. With American influences modeling healthier parent/child relationships, Asians have a different understanding of what it means to be whole. We yearn to find our place in this world and satisfy our souls.

On this journey, many come up short and fall victim to addictions. However, what is unique among Asians is the high degree of shame our cultures have placed on us. I've seen how shame has ravaged my family through gambling, sex, and workaholism.

So why the focus on shame? Because shame at its core leads people to believe they are flawed and defective. Healthy guilt alerts us to behaviors and attitudes that may give rise to concern. For many Asians, the shift from healthy guilt to toxic shame begins early. Because my parents taught my brothers and I that emotions were bad, we never learned how to process them. As a result, when we felt an emotional need or a desire, many of those needs stayed within. Consequently they were never met when we were children.

> To be shame-bound means that whenever you feel any feelings, any need, or any drive you immediately feel ashamed. So as a kid, if you were told it was unacceptable to have feelings, needs, or drives-you were destined to end up shackled in toxic shame. (Bradshaw 1988, 32)

Fast forward to adulthood, and what you find are countless Asians whose emotional lives are clogged up. This emotional repression is the fertile ground for addiction to grow in.

Without a proper place to get their needs met, addicts will turn to other habits. That's the essence of addiction. The substances or the emotional "high" an addiction provides is reliable. The craving for competency and validation can be met through an addiction.

Addictions help take away the pain of feelings of loneliness and unworthiness, and consequently serve as a way to cope with life.

As previously noted, most people erroneously think sex addiction is about sex. But from a psychological or theological standpoint, it's not sex at all. It's about people trying to compensate for their emotional deprivation through sex. It's about trying to overcome the core belief that we are not good enough as human beings.

Asians are most prone to this faulty shame belief system because our cultures encourage:

1. *Performance versus being*
Parents spend an inordinate amount of time focusing on what their children do and miss out on who their children are as people. We become human "doings" instead of human beings.

2. *Conditional love*
When Asian parents do not hug or verbally affirm their children, they are operating out of fear—fear of intimacy, fear of breaking family rules, and so on. This sets up low self-esteem and feelings of abandonment or neglect.

3. *The black hole of the heart*
Believing you have to "do" and achieve leads to the black hole of the heart. No matter how much affirmation addicts receive, they can never get enough. At their cores are black holes that keep demanding more. The vicious cycle of dependency, addiction, and shame goes around and around unless it's broken. And for Asians, breaking the shame means breaking the Asian stronghold of honor, pride, and family.

Chapter 13
Asian Shame And Christianity

"Fortune Cookie Faith"

ASIAN SHAME IS SHARPEST and most crippling when it intersects with Asian Christian churches, which place a high value on religious perfectionism. Our culture and shared heritage bind us together. As Christians, we tell others that our faith is predicated on our belief in God, manifest through Jesus and his teachings. We want Christ elevated, but the reality is that success, looking good, and the perpetuation of the family name prevail in some circles. Few have the courage to heed Christ's calling to worship him over the ingrained cultural priorities of education, success, and family.

Is this really Christ's message? I see so many well-meaning Christians who wonder why they are lackluster in their faith. Well, if we put money, our careers, or our relationships above God, then we will suffer the consequences of a diluted faith. A strong faith is unmistakably built on our security in Christ alone: our children, education, homes, careers, and image are not to be worshipped.

Unfortunately, it is all too common among traditional Asian Christians to pursue what I describe as a "fortune cookie faith." Asians pursue God thinking that this pursuit will lead to more blessings and prosperity. One Chinese Christian I met told me he became a Christian because he believed God wanted to make him a millionaire before he turned thirty-five years old. Can you say "perverted Christianity"?

While God does bless some of us, I think we need to stick to the biblical mandate of putting God first in all things. If thoughts about financial success dominate our lives, for example, then it's likely we have what's known as an "inordinate affection." These affections become distorted because we desire them so much that they supersede our relationship with Christ.

On a similar note, the Christian church can often become a country club in which everyone is doing his or her best to preserve a good image and ignore problems in living. A child is hit. A husband gambles away the family's assets. A mother berates her daughter. An abortion occurs. An extramarital affair is discovered. Yet in many cases these scenarios are brushed over without meaningful discussions during which emotions could be processed, lives healed, and stories of pain redeemed for the kingdom. Instead, real issues with real pain remain hidden under the pretension to keep our honor above all else. This falsehood is so thick in Asian Christian circles that the opportunity for true grace to minister to struggling souls is lost.

Those who are shackled in sexual shame face even more religious challenges. Unlike an addiction to alcohol or drugs, sexual compulsivity isn't easy to understand or embrace. In church circles, the recovering drug addict is encouraged to talk and share about his struggles. However, sex addiction or premarital sex are forbidden secrets. No one wants to hear us talk about our sex lives as it's easy to label it as "dirty", "perverted", or wrong.

But since sex and our sexuality strike at the core of our beings, they are topics that must be discussed, now more than ever before—especially since the media constantly inundates us with sexual images and messages.

Partly to blame is the church's reticence to communicate a message other than that of sexual purity. The church has become a one-trick pony whose only exhortation is "Don't do it!" The church has hidden itself from the hurts of today's sexually broken believers who are desperately looking for true, godly intimacy in relationships. They want and need Christ's message of forgiveness and redemption to be boldly proclaimed. They need a deeper and more thorough understanding to their sexual desires, urges, and deviancies.

Christian author Richard Foster strikingly describes it this way:

> The problem with topless bars and the pornographic literature of our day is not that they emphasize sexuality too much but that they do not emphasize it enough. They totally eliminate relationship and restrain sexuality to the narrow confines of the genital. They have made sex trivial. (Foster 1985, 92)

If churches continue to back away from this central issue, then untold numbers of people will suffer the consequences of this sin of omission. Christian leaders must articulate their faith in the relational covenant of intimacy that God designed between men and women. As it stands, the church is seen as having no relevance in our sex-saturated culture.

With their constant access to new technology, sex permeates the lives of this generation more than ever before. Eighty percent of all 15-17 year olds in the United States have had multiple exposures to hard-core pornography. The revenue for pornography worldwide is $100 billion per year. Online, pornography is the most searched topic, with 68 million hits per day, or 25% of all Internet search engine requests. (Ropelato)

Sex: The Unforgivable Sin?

In church, there are admonitions against sexual immorality, relationships outside of marriage, and even sexual desire. As a result, many Christians equate religious obedience with being asexual. You can see how this creates a shame-filled trap for those struggling with their sexual urges.

Now imagine someone caught in a web of sexual obsessions. Whether it's a preoccupation with a sexual chat room, a one-night stand, multiple affairs, strip clubs, or pornography, the effect of such obsession is that the combined feelings of dirtiness, defectiveness, and weakness race to the forefront. Shame ensnares the entire person and he comes to see himself as unlovable, worthless, and a failure. Unless we tear down the walls of shame, many will suffer in silence and may succumb.

I wish that in the dark days of silence, God's light can shine through the walls of shame and penetrate those hearts. May they soak in God's unfailing love and forgiveness. I know it's there. I've seen and touched it firsthand. The Bible tells us that Christians are in a process of spiritual perseverance called sanctification. "Because of your partnership in the gospel from the first day until now, being confident of this, that he who began a good work in you will carry it on to completion until the day of Christ Jesus" (Philippians 1:5-6 TNIV). I believe this, or I would have drowned in utter hopelessness amidst my own setbacks.

Chapter 14
Shame And Recovery

A Spiritual Journey

ASKING FOR HELP IS hard to do. Even though I sought help during the four years following my divorce, it wasn't a linear process. I fought against it at many points along the way. Everything within me wanted to care for myself. I detested help. I didn't want to join a group of "losers." I believed my struggle was different from theirs. I only relented after enduring further emotional hell. I realized I was powerless to lift myself out of my own addiction, anxiety, and depression cycle.

The swing from anxiety to despair went something like this. I would get anxious or stressed about some aspect of life (i.e. work, relationships), so I would turn to pornography to ease the stress. In doing so, my spiritual life was affected, and I would feel hopeless and depressed about my addiction. Then the stress of depression would drive me to turn to pornography again. This cycle would viciously repeat itself: anxiety, pornography, and depression. Whatever the emotional crisis, I would use porn to get me to a better place emotionally. But the effect was only temporary, and despair and depression would inevitably follow.

I knew I needed help. I needed to surrender my will to God and let him into my life in an earnest attempt to live differently.

While self-awareness is great, therapy can be healing, and small groups can provide accountability, nothing will truly free us from our addictions if we do not have a personal relationship with our

Creator. If we do not learn how to develop intimacy with God and our own humanity, we are destined to remain dependent on our idols. Our addictions must be seen as false intimacy.

To take our idols off center stage, we must surrender those idols to God. We must experience the pain of losing control over the one area of our lives that gave us some semblance of control. It's imperative that we reorient our entire lives: thoughts, emotions, worldviews, habits, hobbies, desires, relationships, money, careers, and time. It's only when we walk this spiritual road that we stand a chance at real change and transformation.

With a Christian understanding of the nature of addiction and how it is really a form of idolatry, we must consider the practical and therapeutic steps necessary for recovery. I like to put recovery under the umbrella of spirituality. I believe everything about the recovery process is soul work. We must learn to commit to a community of people who are willing to hold each other accountable.

Accountability can come from a church, a mentor, or a close friend, but it must be lived out in community. Verbalizing your deepest needs, fears, and concerns to a group is essential. Only when one is exposed and vulnerable within a supportive community can healing and growth occur. Isolation and secrecy are where addictions thrive. Counseling should also be considered if you are uncomfortable with emotional intimacy and are unaware as to what "triggers" or compels you to relapse into your addictive cycle.

The majority of sex addicts have unresolved trauma in their lives. Trauma is more than just physical or sexual abuse. It can come from emotional neglect. A mother or father may have been physically unavailable. It can be a pattern of put-downs. All of these examples can be traumatic if the circumstances result in the belief that one cannot trust people with one's internal world. Part of therapy is the hard work of helping clients process the deep childhood trauma—wounds, hurts, neglect—that drove them to find comfort in pornography.

The Sexual Fantasy: A Path Toward Healing

While online pornography has entangled many addicts, it has also provided much needed information for uncovering deep soul wounds.

An *arousal template* is a blueprint of our sexual belief system that takes into account our life experiences, sexual experiences, and what we are told or learn about sex. The template, which is mostly unconscious, guides us into what we feel is erotic (Carnes 2001-2010)

Almost anything can become part of the arousal template. A rural child growing up where there was no running water might have snuck up behind an outhouse to watch female family members urinate. Curiosity and arousal could then become connected with urination. As an adult, this person might view urination as a cue for arousal (Carnes 2001-2010, 247).

Take as another example a client who spent two hours every day downloading pictures of women in lingerie. At the time he entered treatment, he had more than a hundred CDs full of pictures of women in lingerie. Peeling back the layers in therapy, one discovers that as a youngster, the client was sexually fascinated with lingerie ads he stumbled across in a department store catalog. This man's fixation with lingerie started when he grew up in a family that never talked about sex. The catalog provided his only access to sexual information. (Carnes 2001-2010)

Intimacy Is Possible

I know recovery from sexual addiction is not only possible but life-enriching. It's more than just "sobriety" (i.e. measuring the length of time you haven't looked at pornography or had illicit sex). It's also about sanctification. While my spiritual struggle is comparable to Paul's "thorn in his flesh," I can honestly say I no longer live with the fear of intimacy that drove me to pornography. I do not hide my feelings from God or others. I am as transparent as I can be, and I give God glory for remaking me with a heart to empathize with those who are hurting in this world.

What I've learned from this journey is that the wounds from one's past are real and must be dealt with if one is suffering from an addiction. These wounds cannot simply be dismissed. The core pangs of our hearts are what drive us to fill the holes in our hearts. The loss, hurt, and rebellious spirit within must all be processed so one can grieve and grow into the man or woman God intended.

> Sinful habits become compulsively attractive when the pleasure they give relieves deep disappointment in the soul better than anything else one can imagine. The good feelings offered by having enjoyable sex, eating delicious food, or controlling crowds with skilled oratory can numb the ache of unmet longings by providing satisfaction that, for a time, fulfills like nothing else ever has. (Crabb 1988, 105)

What is the deep disappointment within your soul? How have you used this pain to justify or rationalize past or current behaviors? If you surrendered this to God, how would it feel to be stripped of your need for control?

I remember driving down a dark stretch of highway in Washington one winter day and feeling an intense despair in my soul. The despair wasn't about anything specific, other than the fact that nothing in this life satisfied me: not career, relationship, athletic achievement, wealth, status, or material possession. At that point I realized nothing this side of heaven could fill the vacuum in my heart. I had tried all those other things to fill it, but the stark reality is they all fall short of God's promise of eternity.

As I find more distance from my form of idolatry, I come closer to Christ, knowing I was created for something more—God's desire for me to seek comfort and refuge in him.

> I learn that dreams for good things may shatter, but our pain will always have a purpose. It will not go away, but it will do its work. It will stir an appetite for a higher purpose—the better hope of knowing God well enough

now to love him above everything else and trusting Him no matter what happens. (Crabb 1984, 35)

This is the ultimate test for us. How do we surrender our trust to God? Trust in everything: our sexuality, our finances, our health, our careers, our relationships, our kids, our education, our fears and insecurities, and ultimately our lives to him.

There's no one, magical way to recovery, but I think the path is through God. For those suffering in silence, it's my desire you will someday experience the liberation of feeling God's love and acceptance despite your failings.

Change Of Behavior Or Change Of Heart?

"I'm tired of living the lie."

"It's just about the hit."

"Sex became a huge comfort for me; it became a place of release."

"It's the first thing I think about in the morning and the last thing I think about at night, the end of the day."

"I reward myself with sex."

"My greatest desire is to be clean."

These are some of the statements clients have made to me regarding their sex lives and their desires to change. The hard part as a counselor is that each person is on a different path toward change. Change, as we know, is difficult, for it requires us not only to stop the actions but the accompanying thoughts and feelings associated with those actions.

In helping clients address their desires to change their compulsive and addictive behaviors, I must do more than have them just stop "acting out." Stopping the behavior, while seemingly admirable, is just behavioral modification and doesn't address a true change of the heart.

There's a saying in recovery circles: "white-knuckling it," otherwise known as being a "dry drunk." What this means is an addict such as an alcoholic may quit drinking, but never truly reach sobriety, freedom, or peace from the craving for alcohol. He is still addicted. He "white-knuckles it" (referring to the effect when your knuckles lose their natural color because you have clenched your fist so hard) because even though he has used his own willpower to technically stop drinking, everything within his soul thirsts for alcohol. In many instances the anxiety, hurt, anger, and other powerful emotions that were buried come to forefront during this stage but are never processed and worked through.

Sadly, even though this guy may be "sober" by societal standards, we in the recovery world know differently. His heart has not come to terms with the motivations and hurts that propelled him to his addictive behavior. If I as his therapist neglect to go beyond the behavior, then the counseling is shallow and fails to minister to the heart of the individual.

Take this example of a Christian client who was very legalistic in his understanding of sin, healing, and recovery.

> "Sin is bad. Don't do it. Just do _____ to help you not sin." His entire Christian life was conceived and constructed around this struggle with episodic sexual sin.
>
> His pattern was as follows: Seasons of relative purity might last for days, weeks, even for a few months. He measured his success by "How long since I last fell?" The longer he went, the more his hopes would rise: "Maybe now I've finally broken the back of my besetting sin." Then he would fall again. He would stumble through seasons of defeat, wandering back to the same old pigsty. "Am I even a Christian? Why bother? What's the point? Nothing ever works." He was plagued with guilt, discouragement, despair, and shame. He would turn back to pornography to dull the misery of his guilt over using pornography. He would beg God's forgiveness over and over and over, without any relief or any joy. (Powlison, 2005, 86)

In this case, the client's entire life was centered on his cycle of being "good" or being "bad." What's needed here is an exploration of the entitlement and rage he feels against God.

Erotic motives, the "feel good" of sex, played an important role. But other motives—"I want a wife"; "If I'm good, God owes me goodies"; "I'm angry because God has let me down"—interconnected with his eroticism. Many co-conspirators play a role when he starts rummaging in the gutter of "I want to look at a naked Playmate" and "I need sexual release now." Many other lusts join hands to give a boost to sexual lust. (Powlison, 2005, 90)

When it comes to sex, few people recognize that sex is not just about sex. In fact much more is at play: the feelings of desire, intimacy, power, loneliness, sadness, and completeness are so intertwined that they must also be addressed.

Take the example of a young girl who lacks the love and nurturing of a good father. In an effort to get validation, affirmation, and attention, she lacked from him, she ends up giving herself to boys. She may not have any sexual lust in her heart but barters her body away as a means to get the attention she desperately missed out on in childhood. This girl would be severely shamed if we focused on her behavior without addressing her deep longing for human attention.

Some see sex as a "release" from stress. But it often is nothing more than a mask for deeper issues that they believe cannot be resolved on a relational level and thus get mislabeled as sexual stress. Sex becomes a way of escaping reality and all the burdens of the day. The real stress could be related to work, relationships, unresolved emotions such as anger or loneliness, or a myriad of other reasons that drive one to hide.

Only when the client is willing to be vulnerable, to share his hurts with a counselor, friend, or mentor, can lasting change occur. In order to obtain true and lasting change, we must move beyond external sin and delve deeper into the hidden sins of the heart that often remain unexplored.

This being said, a heavy dose of grace must be offered to those gripped by sexual sin. Miraculous change in one person's life, while making for dramatic testimony, cannot be viewed as the only path of healing. Instead, we must remember the hard reality that, "relapse is a part of recovery" for most addicts. It's wonderful when someone is able to give up an addiction in a once-and-for-all moment of surrender, but that person's testimony cannot set the bar for the rest of us.

In Christianity, one generally hears the amazing testimonies of success and rarely hears the testimony of the millions of hardworking men and women grinding it out, day by day and week by week, often falling short but at the same time having the faith, hope, and courage to get back up and go to battle again. I consider their struggles the hidden struggles of exemplary faith. The struggle to valiantly continue despite occasional setbacks and feelings of shame or ineptitude is the mark of commitment.

I found this process of change best articulated by Christian counselor David Pawlison.

> The key to getting a long view of sanctification is to understand direction. What matters most is not the distance you've covered. It's not the speed you're going. It's not how long you've been a Christian. It's the direction you're heading … the rate of sanctification is completely variable. We cannot predict how it will go. Some people, during some seasons of life, lead and bound like gazelles. Let's say you've been living in flagrant sexual sins. You turn to Christ; the open sins disappear. No more fornication, sleeping with your girlfriend or boyfriend. No more exhibitionism, wearing revealing clothes. No more pornography, buying *Penthouse* or the latest salacious romance novel. Ever. It sometimes happens like that. For other people (and the same people, at another season in life) sanctification is a steady, measured walk. You learn truth. You learn to serve others constructively. You build new disciplines. You learn basic life wisdom. You learn who God is, who you are, how life works. You learn to worship, to pray, to give time, money, and caring. And you grow steadily—wonder of wonders! Other people (and the same people, at another

season) trudge. It's hard going. You limp. You don't seem to get very far very fast. But if you're trudging in the right direction, someday you will see him face to face, and you will be like him. Some people crawl on their hands and knees. Progress is painful. Praise God for the glory of his grace, you are inching in the right direction. And then there are times you aren't even moving, stuck in gridlock, broken down—but you're still facing the right direction ... there are times you wander in the wrong direction, beguiled by some false promise, or disappointed by a true promise that you falsely understood. But he who began a good work in you awakens you from your sleepwalk, sooner or later, and puts you back on the path. And then there are times you revolt, and do a face-plant in the muck, a swan dive into the abyss—but grace picks you up and washes you off again, and turns you back.

We love gazelles. Graceful leaps make for a great testimony to God's wonder-working power. And we like steady and predictable. It seems to vindicate our efforts at making the Christian life work in a businesslike manner. But, in fact, there's no formula, no secret, no technique, no program, and no truth that guarantees the speed, distance, or time frame. On the day you die, you'll still be somewhere in the middle, but hopefully further along. When we lengthen the battle, we realize that our business is in the direction. God manages to work his glory in and through all of the above scenarios! God's people need to know that, so someone else's story doesn't set the bar in a place that is not how your story of Christ's grace is working out in real life. (Powlison, 2005, 82)

Epilogue

AUTHOR AND POET ROBERT Bly says only when we enter our wound will we discover our true glory: "Where a man's wound is, that is where his genius will be" (Bly 1990) There are two reasons why. First, the wound was given to help us let go of our desire to focus on our accomplishments. We trade our strength and power for one of submission and humility—humility that comes from our brokenness and desire to surrender to God's will.

Second, it's our brokenness that gives us a glimpse of what we truly have to offer this world. When we offer more than our self-proclaimed strengths and talents but also our gift of powerlessness and weakness, do our true selves emerge. Only then, do we become truly powerful and transcend our humanity. (Eldredge 2001)

It's quite ironic how true this is for me. As a first-generation Chinese immigrant, I was indoctrinated to bring honor to my family and ancestry while chasing the American dream. But it wasn't until that dream of success, perfection, and independence was obliterated that I had the courage to delve deep into my own cultural wounds of Asian shame and addiction. Only then was I able to find what I was looking for in life: meaning, passion, love, and the joy of experiencing intimacy with God and my fellow man.

I no longer see my faults as bringing shame to my culture, family, or me. Instead, my faults are a chance to showcase God's power of grace—grace that makes good out of our trials, failures, and disappointments. It's this promise God can reveal to you in your own moments of abject fear, humiliation, or hopelessness. May you know in your heart that no matter how desperate the situation or impossible the odds, therein lies the greatest opportunity for spiritual growth, healing, and discovery.

And if you're Asian and your identity is tied to perfection, success, or honor, I leave you with this parable as a reminder that your imperfection is what makes you valuable.

The Legend Of The Cracked Pot

A WATER BEARER IN India had two large pots, one hung on each end of a pole which he carried across his neck and shoulders. One of the pots had a crack in it, and while the other pot was perfect and always delivered a full portion of water at the end of the long walk from the stream to the master's house, the cracked pot arrived only half full.

For two years this was the daily routine, with the water bearer delivering only one and a half pots full of water to his master's house. Of course, the perfect pot was proud of its accomplishments, performing perfectly the reason for which it had been made. On the other hand the cracked pot was ashamed of its own imperfections, and felt itself a failure since it was only capable of accomplishing half the task it had been made to do. The bitterness grew and the cracked pot finally found the courage to speak to the bearer. "I am ashamed of myself, and I want to apologize to you."

"Why?" asked the bearer. "What are you ashamed of?"

"I have failed to fulfill the purpose for which I was made. I am only capable of delivering half the water, because of the crack in my side. You have to do all this work and you do not get full value for your efforts," the pot said.

The water bearer said to the pot, "Have you noticed the flowers that grow alongside of the path? They are there because I planted seeds, knowing that as we walked back up the path your dripping water would nourish them. I have been able to provide flowers for the master's table because of the water that you provided the flowers. Without you being just the way you are, there would have been no time to grow the flowers. You have not failed, your flaws have been put to good use." (author unknown)

References

Pg. 7 - [http://www.who.int/mentalhealth/media/japa.pdf]

Pg. 7 - Condon, John C. 1984. *With Respect to the Japanese*. Yarmouth, Maine: Intercultural Press.

Pg. 7 - Yukiko Nishihara, a Japanese suicide prevention activist and founder of the Tokyo-based chapter of Befrienders Worldwide, offers this cultural explanation to Japanese suicide. "Death puts an end to everything, and the victim becomes a god, and becoming free of criticism". (USA TODAY, 5/29/2007)

Pg. 7 - Yuzo Kato, the director of the Tokyo Suicide Prevention Centre, believes shame and honor play a significant role that contributes to the high suicide rate. "Japan's national character is such that people are socially conditioned to hide their pain, to avoid troubling others by opening up." [http://www.guardian.co.uk/world/2008/jun/19/japan1]

Pg. 8 - USA Today, Suicide Article 5/29/2007

Pg. 8 - In 2007, Japan's agriculture minister Toshikatsu Matsuoka killed himself while facing investigation over an expenses scandal. In response, the governor of Tokyo, Shintaro Ishihara, glorified Matsuoka by stating he was a true samurai because he had committed suicide to preserve his honor.
[http://www.guardian.co.uk/commentisfree/2010/aug/03/japan-honourable-suicide-rate]

Pg. 10 - Dayton, Tian 2000. *Trauma and Addiction: Ending the Cycle of Pain Through Emotional Literacy*. Deerfield Beach, Florida: Health Communications, Inc.

Pg. 11 - McGoldrick, Giordano, Joe & Garcia-Preto, Nydia 2005. *Ethnicity & Family Therapy*, Third Ed., New York, NY: The Guilford Press.

Pg. 12 - Kaufman, Dr. Gershen 1996. *The Psychology of Shame: Theory and Treatment of Shame-Based Syndromes, Second Edition*, New York, NY: Springer Publishing Company, Inc.

Pg. 13 - Halpern, Dr. Howard M. 2004. *How to Break Your Addiction to a Person*, New York, NY: Bantam Books.

Pg. 16 - Kaufman, Dr. Gershen 1996. *The Psychology of Shame: Theory and Treatment of Shame-Based Syndromes, Second Edition*, New York, NY: Springer Publishing Company, Inc.

Pg. 17 - Teyber, Edward 2006. Interpersonal Process in Therapy: An Integrative Model Fifth Edition, Belmont, CA: Thomson Brooks/Cole.

Pg. 22 & 23 - Nakken, Craig 1996. *The Addictive Personality: Understanding the Addictive Process and Compulsive Behavior 2nd Edition*, Center City, MN: Hazelden.

Pg. 24 - Nichols, Dr. Michael 1987. *Turning Forty in the Eighties, Personal Crisis, Time for Change*, New York, NY: Fireside/Simon and Schuster.

Pg. 25 - Bradshaw, John 2005. *Healing the Shame That Binds You*, Deerfield Beach, FL: Health Communications, Inc.

Pg. 37 - Kaufman, Dr. Gershen 1996. *The Psychology of Shame: Theory and Treatment of Shame-Based Syndromes, Second Edition*, New York, NY: Springer Publishing Company, Inc.

Pg. 38 - Kaufman, Dr. Gershen 1996. *The Psychology of Shame: Theory and Treatment of Shame-Based Syndromes, Second Edition*, New York, NY: Springer Publishing Company, Inc.

Pg. 38 - Nakken, Craig 1996. *The Addictive Personality: Understanding the Addictive Process and Compulsive Behavior 2nd Edition*, Center City, MN: Hazelden.

Pg. 39 - Nakken, Craig 1996. *The Addictive Personality: Understanding the Addictive Process and Compulsive Behavior 2nd Edition*, Center City, MN: Hazelden.

Pg. 40 - Carnes, Dr. Patrick 2001. Out of the Shadows: *Understanding Sexual Addiction*, Center City, MN: Hazelden.

Pg. 48 - Kaufman, Dr. Gershen 1996. *The Psychology of Shame: Theory and Treatment of Shame-Based Syndromes, Second Edition*, New York, NY: Springer Publishing Company, Inc.

Pg. 49 - Kaufman, Dr. Gershen 1996. *The Psychology of Shame: Theory and Treatment of Shame-Based Syndromes, Second Edition*, New York, NY: Springer Publishing Company, Inc.

Pg. 54 - Kaufman, Dr. Gershen 1996. *The Psychology of Shame: Theory and Treatment of Shame-Based Syndromes, Second Edition*, New York, NY: Springer Publishing Company, Inc.

Pg. 55 - Bradshaw, John 2005. *Healing the Shame That Binds You*, Deerfield Beach, FL: Health Communications, Inc.

Pg. 55 - Dayton, Tian 2000. *Trauma and Addiction: Ending the Cycle of Pain Through Emotional Literacy.* Deerfield Beach, Florida: Health Communications, Inc.

Pg. 55 - Nichols, Dr. Michael P. 1991. *No Place to Hide: Facing Shame So We Can Find Self-Respect*, New York: Simon & Schuster.

Pg. 55 - Peck, M. Scott 1978. *The Road Less Traveled: A New Psychology of Love, Traditional Values, and Spiritual Growth*, New York, NY: Touchstone.

Pg. 60-61 - Olson, Dr. David & Gorral, Dean 2006. Faces IV and the Circumplex Model (abstract) http://www.facesiv.com/pdf/3.innovations.pdf

Pg. 62 - Carnes, Dr. Patrick 1991. *Don't Call it Love: Recovery From Sexual Addiction*, New York: NY Bantam Books.

Pg. 63 - Olson, Dr. David & Gorral, Dean 2006. "Faces IV and the Circumplex Model" (abstract)

Pg. 65 - Laaser, Dr. Mark 1992. *Faithful and True: Sexual Integrity in a Fallen World,* Grand Rapids, MI: Zondervan.

Pg. 66 & 67 - Mikulincher, Dr. Mario and Shaver, Dr. Phillip 2007. *Attachment in Adulthood: Structure, Dynamics, and Change.* New York, NY: Guilford Press.

Pg. 67 - Bogaert, A. F. and Sadava, S. 2002. *Adult attachment and sexual behavior. Personal Relationships*, 9: 191–204)

Pg. 68- Mikulincher, Dr. Mario and Shaver, Dr. Phillip 2007. *Attachment in Adulthood: Structure, Dynamics, and Change.* New York, NY: Guilford Press

Pg. 68 & 69 - Fraley, Waller, and Brennan 2000. The Experiences in Close Relationships-Revised (ECR-R) Questionnaire

Pg. 69 - For a more exact analysis of your attachment style, you can participate in a free assessment at the Your Personality website, which hosts several questionnaires at www.yourpersonality.net. The relationship questionnaire (http://www.yourpersonality. net/cgi-bin/relationships/getsurvey.pl) is part of a study being conducted by the University of Illinois at Urbana-Champaign and is open to everyone.

Pg. 71 - Denizet-Lewis, Benoit 2009. *America Anonymous: Eight Addicts in Search of a Life,* New York, NY: Simon & Schuster.

Pg. 81 - Ropelato, Jerry, "Internet Pornography Statistics," http:// internet-filter review.toptenreviews.com/internet-pornography-statistics.html (accessed Feb. 20, 2008).

Pg. 82 - Bradshaw, John 1988. *Healing the Shame That Binds You,* Deerfield Beach, FL: Health Communications, Inc.

Pg. 87 - Foster, Richard 1985. *Money, Sex, and Power: The Challenge of the Disciplined Life,* San Francisco, CA: Harper & Row.

Pg. 87 - Ropelato, Jerry, "Internet Pornography Statistics," http:// internet-filter review.toptenreviews.com/internet-pornography-statistics.html (accessed Feb. 20, 2008).

Pg. 91 - Carnes, Dr. Patrick 2003. (Abstract) "The Anatomy of Arousal: Three Internet Portals" Sexual and Relationship Therapy Vol 18, No. 3, August 2003)

Pg. 91 - Carnes, Dr. Patrick 2001-2010. *Facing the Shadow,* Carefree, AZ: Gentle Path.

Pg. 92 - Crabb, Dr. Larry 1988. *Inside Out,* Colorado Springs, CO: NavPress.

Pg. 93 - Crabb, Dr. Larry 1984. *Shattered Dreams: God's Unexpected Path to Joy*, Colorado Springs, CO: Waterbrook Press.

Pg. 94-97 - Powlison, David. "Making All Things New: Restoring Pure Joy to the Sexually Broken." *Sex and the Supremacy of Christ.* Ed. Piper, John and Taylor Justin 2005. Wheaton, IL: Crossway Books, 2005. 64-106.

Pg. 99 - Bly, Robert 1990. *Iron John: A Book About Men* New York, NY: Vintage Books.

Pg. 99 - Eldredge, John 2001. Wild at Heart: Discovering the Secret of a Man's Soul , Nashville, TN: Thomas Nelson.

Scripture quotations noted are from THE HOLY BIBLE: TODAY'S NEW INTERNATIONAL VERSION (TNIV)